new
perennials
the latest and best perennials

new perennials

the latest and best perennials

Jenny Hendy with David Tarrant

WHITECAP BOOKS

Vancouver/Toronto

5132

New Perennials

This edition published in 1999 by

Whitecap Books Ltd., 351 Lynn Avenue

North Vancouver, B.C., Canada V7J 2C4

© 1999 Quadrillion Publishing Limited,

Woolsack Way, Godalming, Surrey, GU7 1XW

United Kingdom.

Canadian Cataloguing in Publication Data

Hendy, Jenny.

New perennials

Includes index.
ISBN 1-55110-821-6

1. Perennials

I. Tarrant, David. II. Title.

SB434.B57 1999   635.9'32   C98-911106-7

Printed in Italy

ISBN 1-55110-821-6

Jacket: A romantic display of roses and perennials.

Page 1: A very modern scheme with artemisia, grasses, knautia and penstemons.

Page 2: An urn forms a focal point in a border with valerian and irises.

Above right: Yellow oenothera with artemisia and blue geraniums.

All text by Jenny Hendy, except the following sections, by David Tarrant:

p16 Happy Accidents

p23 Shady Subject

p27 Dark and Shady

p34 Perennials From Seed

p52 Pink Butterflies

p77 Cold Climate Mulches

p88 Winter Protection.

Credits

Editor: Joanna Smith

Designer: Mark Buckingham

Design Manager: Justina Leitão

Project Editor: Jane Alexander

Artworks: Vana Haggerty

Americanizer: Catriona Tudor Erler

Production: Sandra Dixon, Karen Staff

Production Director: Graeme Proctor

contents

foreword

Perennials are the backbone of any garden, no matter how small a space one is dealing with – whether it's a traditional long perennial border or a tiny city garden. This is an extremely versatile group of plants, coming in all shapes, colors, heights and textures. Many are very happy in containers on small patios or apartment balconies. Perennials defy all hardiness zone guidelines, thriving in places they have no business being, as long as they are planted in well-drained soil and have a good blanket of snow in colder climates.

Sometimes perennials are thought of as low-maintenance plants that need no care once they are planted. That is not quite the case, and this well-written book deals with soil and site preparation as well as all the other on-going maintenance routines that will produce an awe-inspiring perennial bed or border. There are invaluable lists of suitable plants for every possible growing situation, including some complementary plants, such as annuals and shrubs, that work well with perennials in modern mixed borders.

—David Tarrant

Far left: Red valerian, *Centranthus ruber*, seeds itself around, popping up in corners and in cracks between paving stones.

This book is about some of the best perennials available today – those that are popular now as well as some that are ready to become garden classics. It aims to show how incredibly versatile they can be, with individuals to suit even the most difficult and demanding sites.

The term "perennial" covers a whole range of plants from creeping ground cover and compact plants to towering specimens that are almost living sculptures. Some are grown chiefly for their blooms but many have good foliage, occasionally evergreen, that extends their period of interest far beyond the flowering season.

The impressive flower borders of the Victorians and Edwardians were highly labor intensive. Today's plots are often too small to accommodate such extravagant features, and even in large gardens, the busy lifestyles of the owners mean plants have to look after themselves. Gardeners often assume that shrubs are the only option for an easy-care garden, but there are perennials that can remain undisturbed once planted and others that require only infrequent division to keep them flowering well. Staking plants can also be time consuming, but most of the plants in this book are self supporting. Nowadays people are more environmentally aware and reluctant to use chemicals so modern perennials need to have good pest and disease resistance.

Other factors influencing our choice of plants include color. Gardeners are always looking out for more unusual shades and are willing to experiment with bold or subtle schemes that echo interior décor. Form is another factor,

with sculptural shapes becoming more and more popular. Ornamental grasses are a typical example of this trend. And now, after years of scent being bred out of plants in pursuit of such goals as greater flowering performance and a wider color range, fragrant and aromatic plants are now very much back in fashion.

The word "new" in the title refers to plants that have been bred in the last few years or those that have been recently introduced from the wild. It also includes plants that have come back into fashion after a long period of virtual obscurity. In other words, the book is about what's currently in vogue. Fashion in plants is closely related to the prevailing garden styles. For example, with new interest in cottage and romantic gardens, along with period and formal designs, old-fashioned plants are becoming popular once more. Wild gardens and naturalistic plantings are also fashionable so plants that blend easily with wild flowers, or which look wild themselves, are also sought after. And gardeners in low-rainfall areas, particularly those faced with water restrictions, are increasingly turning to Mediterranean-style gravel or paved gardens where planting schemes tend to be quite sculptural as well as aromatic.

introduction

Perennials are the icing on the cake. They dress the garden once the backbone of trees and shrubs is in place, softening hard lines and adding color and texture. Most are grown for their elegant blooms, but others are used for their beautiful, colorful foliage.

Far left: Rheum palmatum 'Atrosanguineum' is a fine example of a perennial grown mainly for its foliage. It enjoys growing at the water's edge, but will also survive in a well-mulched border.

Above: A beautiful wine-red lenten rose (*Helleborus orientalis*).

Right: The soft yellow mullein (*Verbascum chaixii* 'Gainsborough').

Far right: A wonderful herbaceous border in midsummer. *Perovskia* 'Blue Spire' and the globe thistle, *Echinops ritro* 'Veitch's Blue' add blue tones, while *Echinacea purpurea* 'Magnus' and bee balm (*Monarda*) provide rich pink.

The vast majority of the plants mentioned in this book are easy to care for and are top performers with at least two features that make them worth growing. For example, in the case of *Iris foetidissima*, its main features are its evergreen leaves and attractive orange fall berries. But it is also shade and drought tolerant, making it an ideal specimen for planting under trees and shrubs. Many of the plants have won horticultural awards in various countries such as the Award of Gardening Merit given by the British Royal Horticultural Society.

Conditions in different gardens vary so greatly that the only way to know for sure that a particular plant is suitable for you is to have a good look around. Get to know the plants that do well in your neighborhood. Visit gardens open to the public, go to flower shows and join gardening clubs to get specific advice. Sometimes though, you just have to take a chance and often you will discover that you can grow a plant in your garden after all, even though it says the exact opposite in all the reference books you've read.

The formal herbaceous border, a breathtaking sight in June and July, has strong associations with the English style of gardening. The fashion for flower borders started around the mid 19th century but it was Gertrude Jekyll, in partnership with Sir Edwin Lutyens, who perfected the art, using flowers in the border like paint on a canvas. You can still find many fine examples of traditional herbaceous borders in the gardens of historic country houses around Britain. Nowadays, they have been largely superseded by mixed borders which embrace every kind of plant including annuals, hardy and tender perennials, grasses, bulbs, small trees, shrubs and climbers.

It requires a lot of planning and effort to get a border, planted purely with herbaceous perennials, to work visually. Without plants like bulbs and annuals, the season of interest is inevitably quite short and there are likely to be many gaps in flowering. In a mixed border much of the height, structure and year-round interest comes from shrubs including evergreens and small ornamental trees. Most herbaceous plants die back to ground level in winter, leaving borders relatively flat and featureless between late fall and mid-spring. Of course, if your garden is covered in snow for most of that time

herbaceous borders will have greater appeal. You can simply tidy the plants at the end of the season, cover the whole lot over with a thick protective mulch, and wait for the thaw.

Christopher Lloyd, one of this century's gardening greats, is a vociferous exponent of the mixed border. He maintains that all the different kinds of plant help one another visually, and in his garden at Great Dixter, Sussex, England, he is constantly experimenting and coming up with new combinations. Annuals, bulbs and tender perennials feature strongly, and are an important element of the bold and exciting color schemes that are his trademark. But this style of gardening is very intensive at certain times of the year, and many people would not be able to manage the workload by themselves.

The best way to cut down on the amount of time spent looking after your borders is to limit the number of seasonal plants, unless they are self-seeders, and concentrate on low-maintenance shrubs and hardy perennials with a long period of interest. As well as hardy perennials, mixed borders can also include many other elements, including shrubs, annuals, biennials and even tender perennials. Choose a selection of each of them for variation in height, structure, texture and a longer season of interest in your border.

Some shrubs work extremely well in the mixed border because they blend well with perennials, giving a similar impression of floral abundance. Shrubs that flower on current season's growth are particularly useful in cold climates because even if

versatile perennials

Herbaceous plants are incredibly adaptable and can be used in a wide range of locations to produce exciting and colorful effects. Many are grown for their flowers, others for foliage alone. Some are statuesque while others form living carpets.

Far left: Pink phlox and blue eryngium form a backdrop to the purple spires of *Liatris spicata* and purple *Allium spaerocephalon.*

Above: An avenue of columnar yews makes a striking statement rising above the undulating carpet of softly-colored perennials.

they are cut to the ground in winter, they often will bounce back and flower as normal. These plants are also easy to manage because you can control their size by hard pruning, never letting them get too large for their allotted space.

Deciduous foliage shrubs quickly create height and color in the mixed border and, unlike many tall perennials, don't need staking. They have a long season of interest, attractive from the moment the new leaves expand in spring until fall, when many develop interesting tints. Once established, most can be hard pruned to control their size. Cut back to a low framework of branches or, less drastically,

cut back one-third of oldest wood, removing it at the base. This also has the effect of increasing the size and brightness of the leaf.

Some annual and biennial flowers look very much like herbaceous perennials and blend in well in the mixed border. With a few exceptions such as nasturtiums, taller varieties or ones with a more relaxed, open habit and single blooms are a much better option than dwarf, compact types, typical of modern bedding. Seasonal plants are useful for augmenting a particular color scheme and you can add quick spots of concentrated color where it's most needed. Single color selections of a plant almost always

work better than mixtures, though these can be harder to find and are often more expensive because they are more time consuming to produce.

Early-blooming bienniels such as wallflowers and English daisies are useful for filling gaps early in the season, before the main perennial display begins. Others, including mullein, clary sage and evening primrose, flower later in summer.

Many annuals are so easy to raise from seed that you can sow them direct in the border. These are the hardy annuals. Sow small patches at intervals every few weeks from early spring until early summer for a succession of bloom that will last until the first killing frost. Some will even come up in subsequent years, creating excellent and unexpected plant combinations. Other annuals have to be raised under glass in spring in areas that get winter frosts. These are known as half-hardy annuals. They can also be bought from a garden center as young plants. They should be planted out after the last spring frosts. This is because they will not survive low temperatures. They are usually in flower for much longer than the hardier annuals that can be sown straight into the soil.

Tender perennials can also make a valuable contribution to a mixed border. Although these perennials are hardy only in the temperate regions of North America, they are great assets. In colder climates, it is worth growing them in your border as annuals, or planning to overwinter them indoors or in a greenhouse. Most have an extremely long flowering period and some, such as verbena, helichrysum

FLOWERING SHRUBS FOR THE MIXED BORDER

Buddleja davidii

Caryopteris x clandonensis
'Heavenly Blue'

Ceanothus x delileanus
'Gloire de Versailles'

Ceanothus x pallidus
'Marie Simon' and
'Perle Rose'

Ceratostigma willmottianum

Fuchsia, hardy hybrids

Hebe

Hydrangea arborescens
'Annabelle'

Hydrangea macrophylla
Lacecap or Mophead cultivars

Hydrangea paniculata

Hydrangea serrata

Lavandula

Lavatera

Potentilla fruticosa

Rosa, modern
repeat-flowering shrub roses

Spartium junceum

TENDER PERENNIALS FOR MIXED BORDERS

Abutilon

Argyranthemum

Bidens ferulifolia

Canna generalis

Convolvulus sabatius

Dahlia

Diascia

Felicia amelloides

Fuchsia

Helichrysum petiolatum

Heliotropium

Lantana camara

Osteospermum

Pelargonium

Solenostemon (syn. *Coleus*)

Verbena

BIENNIALS FOR MIXED BORDERS

Alcea rosea

Bellis perennis

Campanula media

Cheiranthus cheirei

Dianthus barbatus

Digitalis purpurea albiflora
and 'Excelsior Group'

Eryngium giganteum

Lunaria annua

Matthiola incana

Myosotis

Oenothera biennis

Salvia sclarea turkestanica

Verbascum bombyciferum

Verbascum olympicum

HARDY ANNUALS FOR MIXED BORDERS

Calendula officinalis

Centaurea cyanus

Convolvulus tricolor

Echium 'Blue Bedder'

Eschscholzia californica

Iberis umbellata

Lavatera trimestris

Nigella damascena

Papaver somniferum

Reseda odora

Tropaeolum majus

HALF-HARDY ANNUALS FOR MIXED BORDERS

Antirrhinum majus

Atriplex hortensis rubra

Brachycome iberidifolia

Cleome spinosa

Cosmos 'Sonata Series'

Impatiens walleriana

Mimulus

Nicotiana alata

Penstemon

Petunia hybrida

Rudbeckia hirta

Salvia farinacea 'Strata'

Salvia 'Lady in Red'

Verbena hybrida

Viola

FOLIAGE SHRUBS FOR THE MIXED BORDER

Acer negundo 'Flamingo'

Berberis x ottawensis 'Superba'

Berberis thunbergii 'Rose Glow'

Cornus alba 'Spaethii'

Cornus alba 'Elegantissima'

Cotinus coggygria 'Royal Purple'

Cotinus 'Grace'

Philadelphus coronarius 'Aureus'

Physocarpus opulifolius
'Diabolo', 'Luteus' and
'Dart's Gold'

Rosa glauca

Sambucus nigra 'Guincho
Purple' and 'Marginata'

Left: A bright, modern planting, using an imaginative mix of shrubs, climbers and perennials. A glazed pot filled with cerise pink verbena adds punch.

Above: This border, pictured in midsummer, uses a range of different plant types, including shrubs such as the pink lavatera, and tender perennials, as well as hardy perennials. The flowering times of the plants are staggered, so the border provides interest from spring until fall.

Right: Zantedeschia aethiopica has beautifully-sculpted blooms and handsome foliage and is a striking specimen for the bog garden.

Far right: Large swathes of blue irises and orange euphorbia grow in a bog garden alongside a pool.

and bidens, make vigorous front-of-the-border ground covers. Tender perennials often give a subtropical feel too, with vivid colors and eye-catching foliage. Dahlias, cannas, fuchsias and abutilons are good examples.

Unlike bulbs in bedding displays, which are lifted at the end of each season, bulbs in the mixed border can stay put, provided they are hardy. This includes tulips, which in most cases survive quite happily if left in the border. The dwarf cultivars of *Tulipa greigii*, *T. kaufmanniana* and *T. fosteriana*, including the white 'Purissima', are particularly successful.

Leaving bulbs in place makes for a lot less work, but you have to find a way to camouflage the dying leaves. The newly-emerging foliage of many perennials is ideal for this purpose. The leaves of dwarf daffodils such as 'Tête à Tête' and the *cyclamineus* cultivars such as 'Jenny' and 'February Gold' rarely present a problem.

Early dwarf bulbs such as *Crocus chrysanthus* cultivars, scilla and *Iris reticulata* hybrids are useful for filling gaps in borders in early spring. These gaps, as well as the dying bulb foliage, will be covered by the spreading foliage of perennials such as geraniums later in the season.

Summer-flowering bulbs, including hybrid lilies, drumstick alliums and, in a sheltered position, foxtail lilies (*Eremurus*), are ideal for planting in clumps to rise up among surrounding plants in a mixed border. Many of the newer hybrid lilies do not require staking, which is a bonus, and some have a lovely fragrance.

WINTER STRUCTURE

Provided you have a proportion of evergreens, shrubs and trees grown for their attractive stems and bark and a few winter flowers and berries, a mixed border can continue to be attractive beyond fall. The mummified stems and seedheads of several perennial plants, especially grasses, look magical when covered in hoar frost and can help protect the crowns from cold, so don't be in too much of a hurry to cut everything down to ground level in the fall.

Clipped formal hedges that have acted as a backdrop for flowers during the summer take on a new lease of life in winter giving a crisp three-dimensional structure to the garden. Low evergreen hedges help to demarcate the border edge; dwarf box (*Buxus sempervirens* 'Suffruticosa') and lavender cotton (*Santolina chamaecyparissus*) are particularly good for this.

Certain perennials also can be used in this way, producing a more informal effect. One of the best is bergenia with its large, rounded, evergreen leaves that in some varieties take on attractive winter tints. It provides continuity through the year, while surrounding plants ebb and flow. The lily turf (*Liriope muscari*), with grassy foliage and fall flowers, also works well. And for something out of the ordinary, try black-leaved *Ophiopogon planiscapus* 'Nigrescens' or the variegated *Carex oshimensis* 'Evergold'.

HAPPY ACCIDENTS

The addition of annuals to a perennial border can be the spark that really brings it to life, and one of the best is Papaver rhoeas, *more commonly known as the Shirley poppy. These poppies freely seed themselves from year to year. When they germinate next to a clump of frothy white gypsophila or the silver foliage of eryngium, it makes a stunning combination for which the gardener gets all the credit when in fact it is a happy accident of nature.*

*Another stunning combination of annuals and perennials is the vibrant orange California poppy (*Eschscholzia californica*) self-seeded among perennial flax (*Linum perenne*), which has lots of delicate, sky-blue flowers.*

THE BOG GARDEN

Although perennials generally prefer free drainage, most also relish moisture-retentive soil, especially in summer, and dry spells cause growth to slow down considerably. In a bog garden, the soil is constantly moist with occasional water logging. A surprisingly large number of plants tolerate these conditions while others thrive in them. Bog garden plants are characterized by lush growth and often have large architectural leaves that work well next to water or wooden decking. You

can grow some of these plants in an ordinary border situation, but they then need shade and a heavy mulch to reduce water loss. Herbaceous bog plants are useful in cold climates where heavy snow falls preclude the use of tender large-leaved shrubs, by creating height and strong foliage interest in a single season. Bog plants do need shelter, however, as the large foliage will be damaged in a windy site.

Even if you don't have a pond or stream, bog gardens can give the illusion that water is close by. Create the illusion of a pool of water by placing bog plants around a centerpiece of rounded boulders and cobbles. With the aid of a small submersible pump and underground reservoir, you could even create a spring bubbling up from the stones. Both of these options are completely child safe.

If your land isn't naturally boggy, you can create the right conditions. Excavate the soil 12 to 18 inches deep and line the hole with heavy plastic. Punch drain holes in the plastic about every three feet, and then top with a 2-inch layer of lime-free grit or gravel. Refill the hole with a good-quality soil mix such as 3 parts topsoil, 3 parts peat, and 1 part lime. Your aim is to create a growing medium that is both free draining and water retentive. Arrange a decorative border of stones or pebbles to hide the plastic edges. Saturate the bed with water before you plant. During drought periods, keep the soil from drying completely.

Choose a selection of plants with different forms and textures, concentrating on architectural foliage first and adding highlights in the form of strongly-colored flowers.

PERENNIALS FOR A BOG GARDEN

Ajuga reptans
Astilbe
Astilboides tabularis
Carex elata 'Aurea'
Cimicifuga
Darmera peltata
Euphorbia griffithii
Hemerocallis
Hosta
Houttuynia cordata 'Chameleon'
Inula magnifica
Iris chrysographes
Iris ensata
Ligularia dentata 'Desdemona'
Ligularia 'Gregynog Gold'
Ligularia 'The Rocket'
Lysimachia nummularia 'Aurea'
Matteuccia struthiopteris
Mentha suaveolens 'Variegata'
Onoclea sensibilis
Osmunda regalis
Persicaria bistorta 'Superba'
Rheum palmatum 'Atrosanguineum'
Rodgersia
Zantedeschia aethiopica

THE GRAVEL GARDEN

This is an excellent treatment for sunny, dry areas and can be used to create the illusion of a much warmer climate. The word "Mediterranean" frequently is used to describe this type of garden. The layout is usually very informal and the ground is mulched with a layer of gravel or stone chippings. Large rocks or boulders and flat slices of rock that act as stepping stones add textural variety.

Characteristically, the plants that thrive in such hot spots are drought-tolerant silver, grey or blue-leaved plants, succulents and alpines. A few large terracotta pots and sculptural plants like yucca, blue African lily, sea holly, New Zealand flax and red hot poker will enhance the feel.

Aroma is very much part of the Mediterranean garden; the heat that accumulates during the day helps to release aromatic oils into the air. Make the most of this by mixing in shrubby herbs like lavender, rosemary and santolina.

An alternative way to create a Mediterranean garden is to plant in spaces between random paving, for example on a sunny terrace next to the house. It's often possible to over-winter frost-tender plants in such a situation because the paving and walls act as a heat sink, radiating warmth back onto the plants at night.

In recent years, gravel gardens have become a popular way to display ornamental grasses. For more visual interest, combine the grasses with plants that have a completely different habit to create pleasing contrasts. Try bear's breeches (*Acanthus*), elephant's ears (*Bergenia*) and *Sedum*

Left: Groups of armeria and catmint are scattered across the expanse of gravel, as if they seeded themselves there. The color scheme is one of soft pastels with hardy geraniums, alchemilla, and rock roses (*Helianthemum*) planted around the margin.

Right: With their glossy leaves and bold, fleshy flowers, bergenias look well growing through a gravel mulch.

spectabile. Different kinds of grasses look wonderful planted in large interlocking swathes with stretches of clear gravel as contrast. Try to avoid the collector's garden look with one of everything spread out in the gravel. To a large degree, gravel gardens are supposed to mimic nature, and this bitty arrangement is far from natural.

In coastal gardens you can use gravel or small pebbles (as opposed to chippings) and pieces of driftwood to create a kind of beach effect. In seaside gardens, choose plants that can tolerate the salt-laden air and high winds. Use soft, subtle colors – silver-leaved plants with blue, mauve, white or lime green flowers look the most natural. Try sea holly (*Eryngium*), sea kale (*Crambe maritima*), euphorbias, *Rhodanthemum* and hardy geraniums.

Contemplative Japanese gardens also utilize gravel and rock, but the planting tends toward shades of green with foliage plants giving year-round continuity. Dwarf pines and prostrate junipers have a suitably oriental feel, and are drought tolerant once established so make useful structure plants for full sun. In shady areas you could also use Kurume azaleas, ornamental

sedges, ferns and hostas – all do well in partial shade with plenty of organic matter mixed into the soil. Many ferns tolerate dry conditions including *Polystichum*, *Asplenium*, *Dryopteris filix-mas* and *Polypodium*.

MAKING A GRAVEL GARDEN

The main drawback to using gravel as a surface mulch is that it makes a very effective seed bed. So, not only do desirable plants self-seed, but also weeds. Avoid using vigorous ornamentals like lady's mantle (*Alchemilla mollis*) whose offspring will swamp other plants and colonize pathways. You can't use a hoe, so weeding is all by hand except on pathways where you can use a herbicide. In gravel it's difficult to get hold of small seedlings to pull them out, but early treatment is important because smaller plants have relatively little soil attached to their roots and every time you bring fresh soil up to the surface, you get a fresh crop of weeds too. As a rule, the deeper the gravel, the fewer the weeds. This is fine for planted areas, but for pathways it's best to use compacted hard-core as a base and then a relatively thin surfacing of gravel to give a nice firm surface to walk on. The best approach for reducing the weed problem is to prepare the soil for planting, remove perennial weed roots, and then to lay a permeable membrane over the whole area (see page 88). This material has been used in the nursery trade for years, but is now available in garden centers. It prevents root penetration whilst allowing water to seep through to the soil below. It doesn't last forever, however, and weeds will eventually appear.

GRAVEL GARDEN PLANTS

Acaena saccaticupula 'Blue Haze'
Agapanthus*
Armeria maritima*
Artemisia*
Ballota
Bergenia*
Calamintha nepeta
Centranthus ruber*
Convolvulus sabatius*
Crambe maritima*
Diascia
Echinops*
Erigeron karvinskianus*
Eryngium*
Euphorbia*
Festuca glauca*
Geranium cinereum*
Geranium renardii*
Helictotrichon sempervirens*
Iris*
Kniphofia*
Liatris spicata
Libertia*
Nectaroscordum*
Nepeta x faassenii
Oenothera*
Ophiopogon planiscapus 'Nigrescens'
Origanum laevigatum*
Osteospermum jucundum*
Perovskia 'Blue Spire'*
Phlomis
Phuopsis stylosa
Rhodanthemum hosmariense*
Salvia officinalis*
Sedum*
Sempervivum*
Stachys byzantina*
Stipa gigantea
Thymus*
Verbascum
Verbena bonariensis

* denotes suitable for coast gardens

PERENNIALS WITH A COTTAGE GARDEN FEEL

*Achillea**

Alchemilla mollis

*Allium schoenoprasum**

Anemone hybrida and *hupehensis**

Anthemis tinctoria

*Artemisia**

Aster x *frikartii* 'Mönch'*

Astrantia

*Calamintha nepeta**

*Campanula**

Chaerophyllum hirsutum 'Roseum'

*Cynara cardunculus**

Diascia rigescens

Dicentra spectabilis

*Erigeron karvinskianus**

*Eryngium**

Foeniculum vulgare 'Purpureum'

*Geranium**

Hemerocallis

*Hesperis matronalis**

*Knautia macedonica**

Lamium maculatum

Leucanthemum x *superbum**

Malva moschata 'Alba'*

*Mentha**

*Monarda**

Nepeta x *faassenii**

*Oenothera fruticosa**

*Origanum**

Paeonia

Penstemon

Platycodon grandiflorus

*Polemonium caeruleum**

Saxifraga x *urbium**

Scabiosa 'Butterfly Blue'*

*Stachys byzantina**

*Verbascum**

*Verbena bonariensis**

* denotes attractive to bees and butterflies

THE COTTAGE GARDEN

Herbaceous perennials have long been associated with the cottage garden. Everyone recognizes the classic cottage flowers such as delphiniums, lupines and columbine (*Aquilegia*), but it's more the style of garden and the way that plants are used that produces the familiar signature.

First of all, you don't need to live in a cottage to have a cottage garden. But you do need a strong, simple ground plan, perhaps outlined with clipped hedging, otherwise the garden will disappear under a mass of flower and foliage. The planting has to be exuberant with all kinds of plants thrown together in a seemingly haphazard way. Of course this look needs planning and doesn't just happen by accident, so it's useful to know a little of the background to cottage gardening before you begin planting.

In the days of the poor cottager, land was at a premium and vegetables, fruit, medicinal and culinary herbs

Right: Self-seeders, including mullein, dusty miller, opium poppies and foxgloves, help to create a relaxed, haphazard effect, typical of the cottage garden.

Below: This cottage garden is an exuberant mix — mainly herbs, old-fashioned perennials and annuals. The gardener only grows plants that are useful, including those that are edible, aromatic or suitable for cutting.

were all grown together around a dwelling that was often shared with livestock. They didn't waste space on wide paths and patios, lawns or ornamental pools — every inch counted. Bees were kept for honey, candle wax, and for crop pollination. Therefore the plants that bees foraged on were important. Fragrant plants countered the smell of the animals and the privy and were also dried for use indoors. The only real concession to ornament was the introduction of wild flowers such as primroses, violets, musk mallow, snowdrops and bluebells. Also gathered from the countryside were fragrant climbers like the woodbine (*Lonicera periclymenum*) and sweet briar (*Rosa rubiginosa*) which gives off a delicious apple aroma whenever the foliage is disturbed.

In a way, the cottagers were ahead of their time. Today many of us have small plots and garden with a mixture of plants — annuals, perennials, bulbs, shrubs and trees — and with the rise of organic gardening, it has become much more acceptable to grow food crops along with flowers to reduce pest problems. And of course many vegetables and fruit also can be highly ornamental in the garden.

Cottage gardens are often described as being a riot of color. It's not that color scheming isn't important, but bright primary colors have just as much of a role to play as soft pastels. It's up to you to decide how far to turn up the volume.

Apart from clipped hedges, there's not much sculptural planting in the cottage garden so the architectural form of plants like cardoon and angelica becomes important, giving contrast to the amorphous froth of flower. Floriferous really is the key word, but don't get too carried away and forget about foliage when making your selection. Remember, leaves are far more enduring than the blooms.

Plants that still show something of their wild ancestry are favored over highly-bred types so, for instance, go for single blooms and avoid dwarf, compact cultivars. These "improved" forms have often lost their fragrance in the process as well as their grace and simple beauty. Single flowers are also usually more attractive to bees and butterflies and where nectar-rich flowers are attracting insects, that will in turn encourage birds and foraging dragonflies into the garden.

PERENNIALS IN CONTAINERS

Some hardy herbaceous perennials last as long in flower as bedding and so-called patio plants. The more compact forms are therefore ideal for container gardening. There are many good foliage cultivars too that can be combined with seasonal flowers to create a refreshingly-original look.

In areas with cold or wet winters, you can grow more vulnerable peren-nials in pots and move them under cover for the winter. This might include plants like agapanthus, *Convolvulus sabatius*, penstemons and diascias, among others.

There are several ways to use perennials in pots. One is to stick to hardy perennials interplanted with some dwarf bulbs for early seasonal color. Provided you use perennials and alpines that don't need frequent division, maintenance will be kept to a minimum. Use a high proportion of evergreens and you'll ensure year round interest too. Some perennials look good as a single planting: aga-panthus, hostas and ostrich ferns, for example. Others are best confined to a container because they tend to "run." *Houttuynia cordata* 'Chameleon' is a perfect example. With its pretty heart-shaped leaves painted pink,

the season, you can dismantle the arrangement, salvaging the perennials, and potting them up or returning them to the garden to use again the following year. Alternatively, keep them in place and just swap the faded annuals with fresh material.

Whatever technique you favor, perennials give an interesting twist to container gardening. In addition, some will withstand occasional drought, while others are tolerant of shade, so there are also practical reasons for using hardy perennials in your containers.

Left: Some perennials benefit from being pot grown, such as these immaculate hostas, whose leaves are free from slug damage. The variegated ground elder is a better-behaved cousin of the well-known weed.

Above: Potted ferns, blue-flowered violas and ivies make a lovely tiered display on these shady steps.

Right: This pink diascia makes a wonderful contrast to the blue-painted door behind. Raise trailing plants off the ground to show them to their best advantage.

green and pale yellow, and sap that smells of Seville oranges, it's tempting to let it loose in the border, but on moist soil it will spread into everything. In a container, however, provided it is watered and fed regularly and gets some sunshine during the day, it will be beautiful and well behaved.

Another approach is to mix perennials with annuals and other tender plants and simply use the perennials as temporary elements. At the end of

SHADY SUBJECT

An often overlooked but invaluable late summer-flowering perennial for a container in shade is Begonia grandis. It comes to us from China and Japan and looks very much like the indoor houseplant, angel-wing begonia. The foliage is very showy, with deep red veins on the undersides of the leaves that show up well against the green leaf surface. It is very

effective seen in the late afternoon summer sunshine. The flowers are small but they grow in clusters and are bright pink. It likes a woodland-type soil with plenty of leafmold, and it really enjoys a position where it gets some morning sun but good afternoon shade. Many books refer to this plant as an annual or biennial, but it has proven to be truly perennial in the mild Pacific Northwest.

FOLIAGE PERENNIALS FOR CONTAINERS

Silvers, Blues and Greys
Acaena saccaticupula 'Blue Haze'
Artemisia
Festuca glauca
Helictotrichon sempervirens
Hosta
Sempervivum
Stachys byzantina 'Silver Carpet'
Thymus

Purples and Pinks
Ajuga reptans
Euphorbia dulcis 'Chameleon'
Heuchera
Houttuynia cordata 'Chameleon'
Ophiopogon planiscapus 'Nigrescens'
Salvia officinalis
'Purpurascens Group'
Sedum
Viola labradorica

Lime Green and Yellow
Alchemilla mollis
Ballota 'All Hallow's Green'
Carex oshimensis 'Evergold'
Hakonechloa macra 'Aureola'
Hosta
Lysimachia nummularia 'Aurea'
Mentha x gracilis 'Variegata'
Origanum vulgare 'Aureum'
Pleioblastus auricomus
Salvia officianalis 'Icterina'
Thymus

Green or White-variegated
Bergenia
Dryopteris
Euphorbia myrsinites
Holcus mollis 'Albovariegatus'
Iris foetidissima 'Variegata'
Mentha suaveolens 'Variegata'
Polypodium vulgare

PERENNIALS FOR A SHADY GARDEN

Aconitum

Actaea

Ajuga reptans

Alchemilla mollis

Anemone

Arum italicum italicum 'Marmoratum'

Aruncus dioicus

Astrantia

Bergenia

Brunnera macrophylla

Campanula

Chaerophyllum hirsutum 'Roseum'

Corydalis

Dicentra

Doronicum

Epimedium

Euphorbia amygdaloides robbiae

Ferns

Geranium

Hakonechloa macra

Helleborus

x Heucherella

Holcus mollis 'Albovariegatus'

Hosta

Iris foetidissima

Lamium maculatum

Liriope muscari

Milium effusum 'Aureum'

Ophiopogon

Persicaria bistorta

Pleioblastus auricomus

Pulmonaria

Rodgersia

Saxifraga x urbium

Symphytum

Tiarella cordifolia

Tolmiea menzesii 'Taff's Gold'

Tricyrtis

Veratrum

Viola

PERENNIALS FOR SHADE

However sunny your garden is, there will always be areas that receive little direct light either because of shade cast by buildings and fences or by trees and other plants.

Pale-colored flowers and white or yellow-variegated foliage transform a shady spot, and contrary to what you might think, there are plenty of very good plants that thrive in the half light. In particular, many bulbs and herbaceous perennials are shade tolerant. Herbaceous plants are very versatile and you can often get away with growing moisture-loving types

Below: Ostrich ferns, *Matteuccia struthiopteris*, make a sculptural display in front of pink rhododendrons in late spring. English bluebells add a note of rich blue.

Right: Hostas, *Euphorbia griffithii* 'Fireglow' and yellow *Milium effusum* 'Aureum' in a dazzling shade scheme.

Below right: Clumps of deep red dicentra and *Corydalis flexuosa* 'China Blue' are punctuated by rich yellow cowslips (*Primula veris*).

on average, well-drained soil, simply by growing them out of the wilting rays of direct sunlight.

The only problem is that most of the shade-loving plants have evolved in deciduous woodland, and bloom in early spring before the leaf canopy has fully developed overhead, making use of the short spell of direct sunlight at this time of year. This means that shade gardens are usually at their best from late winter to early summer, after which they go into a quiet phase until the fall. You can supplement the color in summer with a whole host of variegated or gold-leaved plants and ferns in rich shades of green, many with architectural qualities. For brighter color, try shade-tolerant bedding plants such as colorful impatiens, begonias, tobacco plants (*Nicotiana*), and some of the many shrubs that will tolerate shady conditions, such as the different kinds of hydrangea.

LIVING CARPETS

You can make virtually any perennial act as ground cover if you set the plants close. But if you have large areas to cover, this could turn out to be expensive. Ideally a ground-cover plant needs to spread readily while still maintaining a dense foliage canopy. Leaf cover not only swamps out weeds, it also retains soil moisture.

Ground cover is synonymous with low-maintenance gardening. It's a great solution for areas where grass won't grow, due to shade for example, or for any areas that are difficult to access or to garden conventionally, such as steep banks. Ground cover is also used in places where people don't want to garden intensively, for example in a very public front garden that's mainly used for parking.

Ground cover has the reputation of being unimaginative, but it need not be dull. Mix together contrasting foliage and flower to create a colorful living tapestry. Underplant with bulbs to extend the season of interest in spring and fall, and vary the texture using upright plants to grow through low spreading types, such as variegated Gladdon iris (*Iris foetidissima* 'Variegata') with *Alchemilla mollis*.

We often imagine ground cover as a low carpet, but you can adjust the height and texture of adjacent blocks to create either gentle undulations or dramatic high-low contrasts. Ornamental grasses can be most effective when used in this way.

Right: Euphorbia cyparissias 'Clarice Howard' flowers in late spring, but the bracts persist through summer. The interweaving of pale flowers creates an interesting contrast with the feathery foliage. This is a great plant for ground cover on light sandy soil in full sun.

Above far right: Silver-leaved deadnettles, such as *Lamium maculatum* 'Pink Pewter' are useful for carpeting shady areas. Grow on moisture-retentive ground to suppress weeds.

You'll get much better results if you're willing to give plants a helping hand on difficult terrain. For the conditions just described, for example, mulch heavily with moisture-retentive organic matter such as well-rotted animal manure. This will give the plants something good to root into. Apply a granular, slow-release fertilizer and water thoroughly during dry spells. Just because the plants are sold as "tough customers" doesn't mean you can just abandon them! Once they are growing in earnest, maintenance may consist of shearing off old foliage to rejuvenate plants midseason. Most are so vigorous that they bounce back surprisingly quickly and some, such as deadnettles, will even produce a fresh crop of flowers. Water thoroughly and apply liquid fertilizer to encouarge regrowth.

When covering ground beneath newly-planted trees and shrubs, keep a clear area around the base of each tree or shrub. Competition from ground cover affects the rate of growth. Fill the gaps with chipped bark to suppress weeds and to help set off the foliage.

Some plants are rampant thugs and are wholly unsuitable for planting in the mixed border, but as ground cover they are unparalleled. Take the dazzling, white-variegated grass, *Phalaris arundinacea* 'Picta'. In moist soil in particular it romps away. It will even travel under paving to come up through the cracks. But you can forget its faults when you see it gleaming in dappled shade as a ground cover.

Many of these problem plants come in useful for colonizing difficult areas where their spread is contained, such as in a narrow bed bordered by a wall or fence on one side and paving, concrete or tarmac on the other. Here strong carpeters such as the mauve-pink hardy geranium (*Geranium x cantabrigiense*) are ideal.

Dry, rooty, and often impoverished soil beneath mature trees can be one of the most difficult areas to manage but here again perennials provide solutions. One of the best is the wood spurge (*Euphorbia amygdaloides robbiae*), another is yellow archangel (*Lamium galeobdolon*). For textural contrast with either use the spiky-leaved *Iris foetidissima*.

VIGOROUS SPREADERS

Ajuga reptans 'Catlin's Giant', 'Jungle Beauty', 'Atropurpurea' and 'Braunherz'

Alchemilla mollis

Campanula portenschlagiana

Campanula poscharskyana 'Stella'

Darmera peltata

Euphorbia amygdaloides robbiae

Euphorbia cyparissias

Geranium x cantabrigiense

Geranium macrorrhizum

Geranium x oxonianum

Lamium galeobdolon

Lamium maculatum

Lysimachia nummularia

Osteospermum jucundum

Phalaris arundinacia 'Picta'

Sedum acre

Sedum spathulifolium

Sedum spurium

Stachys byzantina

Symphytum 'Hidcote Pink' and 'Hidcote Blue'

Tiarella cordifolia

Viola cornuta

Viola labradorica

DARK AND SHADY

The lovely Ophiopogon planiscapus *'Nigrescens' is a popular and relatively new introduction which, in the right location, will send up delicate little pinkish-white blossoms above its black grassy foliage. It forms a good ground cover for light shade. Combine it with* Arum maculatum. *In the fall, when the arum foliage dies back, its brilliant orange berries are displayed against the black ophiopogon foliage.*

PERENNIALS FOR EDGING

Edging is essentially a formal design feature, because you are planting in a line to define an area rather than in random patches. But edging becomes more or less formal depending on the choice of plant and how it's used. Some have quite a loose habit and produce a relaxed effect, with one plant merging into another. A good example is catmint. Others, such as small tussock-forming grasses and sea pink (*Armeria maritima*), are neater, and a wobble in a single line planting sticks out like a sore thumb. With these plants you can strengthen the line by using a double row and staggering the planting.

Larger, bushy or more upright plants create low hedges when planted in a line and summer-flowering kinds are particularly useful for livening up shrub borders planted with evergreens and spring-flowering shrubs. Examples are the tall-growing catmint *Nepeta* 'Six Hills Giant', agapanthus and daylily. Evergreen edgers such as bergenia and purple-leaved heuchera are ideal for mixed borders, the plain leaves acting as a foil for the flowers and helping to provide continuity through the year.

Where a border is edged by a wide paved or gravel path, you can soften the margins using plants that arch over or grow out across the surface such as *Salvia officinalis* 'Purpurascens' and creeping stonecrops like *Sedum* 'Bertram Anderson'. Common marjoram (*Origanum vulgare*) and the daisy-flowered fleabane (*Erigeron karvinskianus*) self-seed readily. They favor the drier border edges, and create a lovely cottage-garden feel.

Left: The bronze leaves of *Heuchera micrantha diversifolia* 'Palace Purple' make a striking edging to this border, filled with orange, red and yellow flowers. The frothy blooms appear in summer, but the foliage Is the main feature.

Above: Many hardy geraniums make excellent edgers with attractive leaves and abundant blooms. Some, like *Geranium* x *riversleaianum* 'Mavis Simpson' flower all summer long.

Right: Sedum aizoon makes a good edging for a hot, dry spot, the fleshy green leaves making a good foil for the red stems and golden yellow blooms.

Many plants can also be used as an edging down both sides of a path. In a woodland setting on either side of a boardwalk, say, you could use airy grasses, such as tufted hair grass (*Deschampsia*) or purple moor grass (*Molinia caerulea*). In an Eastern style or minimalist garden, try ever-green plants with an oriental feel such as Japananese sedge grass (*Carex oshimensis* 'Evergold'), the striking black-leaved *Ophiopogon planiscapus* 'Nigrescens' and lily turf (*Liriope muscari*). And for bordering a narrow pathway in shade try x *Heucherella alba* 'Bridget Bloom' or London pride (*Saxifraga* x *urbium*).

To edge a border around the sides of a sunny patio or terrace that you use for sitting out in summer, you'll need to select a plant with plenty of flower power. Try the pink-flowered *Penstemon* 'Evelyn', delicate *Diascia rigescens*, the daisy-flowered *Osteo-spermum jucundum*, or the fragrant yellow-flowered *Oenothera fruticosa* 'Fyrverkeri' (syn. 'Fireworks').

EDGING PLANTS

Agapanthus

Alchemilla mollis

Allium shoenoprasum

Armeria maritima

Bergenia

Carex buchananii

Carex oshimensis 'Evergold'

Deschampsia caespitosa

Diascia rigescens

Erigeron karvinskianus

Festuca glauca

Geranium

Hakonechloa macra 'Aureola'

Helictotrichon sempervirens

Hemerocallis 'Stella de Oro'

Heuchera

Liriope muscari

Molinia caerulea 'Variegata'

Nepeta

Oenothera

Ophiopogon planiscapus 'Nigrescens'

Origanum

Osteospermum jucundum

Pennisetum orientale

Penstemon 'Evelyn'

Phuopsis stylosa

Salvia officinalis

Saxifraga x *urbium*

Sedum 'Herbstfreude' (syn. 'Autumn Joy')

Sedum telephium maximum 'Atropurpureum'

Stachys byzantina

Tolmiea menzesii 'Taff's Gold'

Viola cornuta

It's important to know as much as you possibly can about a garden, or new area, before deciding what to plant there or beginning any work. The first thing to do is to start by asking yourself the following questions:

How much direct sun does the bed, or each area of the garden, get during the day and at what times of day? If there's very little light you'll need to stick to shade-loving perennials.

Is it windy or sheltered? If the site is very exposed, choose wind-tolerant varieties and avoid large-leaved and brittle-stemmed plants. You may also think about whether there is anything you can do to reduce the wind. Salt spray in coastal areas is also damaging to some plants so you will need to choose with care.

What is the soil like with regard to texture, depth, fertility, drainage and pH (whether it is acidic or alkaline)? Few of us are blessed with ideal deep, fertile, moisture-retentive, free-draining loam, but you can do much to make up for this by choosing plants that suit the conditions you can offer. Poor, dry, stony soils in full sun suit plants that need good drainage such as many of the silver-leaved plants like artemisias and glaucous grasses. Heavy, sticky clay, prone to water-logging in winter but which bakes like concrete in summer, suits a completely different set of perennials, often plants with an indestructible root system. All problem soils can be improved to a certain extent, but it's much better to grow plants that suit the prevailing conditions than to go to a lot of extra effort to ensure the survival of something that's inherently unsuitable for your area.

planning and planting

Successful gardening requires careful planning, beginning with a firm framework. The temptation is to start planting straight away, but you will only end up moving things. And by researching the conditions carefully, you'll avoid making mistakes.

What is the minimum temperature for your area? Make sure that the majority of perennials you choose are sufficiently hardy, otherwise you could waste a lot of money replacing them every year. Lifting rootstocks to protect them under glass or taking overwintering cuttings takes time, but may be worthwhile for certain choice varieties that you cannot resist.

Approximately when are the first and last likely frost dates of the year? This determines the length of your growing season. It's no use planting fall and winter-interest borders if hard frosts spoil the display before it's even got going or if the whole garden is covered by a blanket of snow for months on end.

Is your garden in a frost pocket? This happens on low ground where cold air collects and is unable to escape. Frost is likely to be more severe here than in surrounding areas and will shorten the growing season considerably.

Don't despair if at first sight your garden seems to present all kinds of problems. Nearly everyone's does. But there are many different perennials to suit any situation and, unlike shrubs, many of them are very adaptable and will happily grow in a wide range of circumstances. Consult the directory section of this book to check on their suitability before purchase.

Far left: Golden hostas, blue nepeta and pink geraniums combine with the yellow-leaved tree *Catalpa bignonioides* 'Aurea' and the biennial *Salvia sclarea turkestanica* behind. Many of these plants have large leaves so a scheme like this would need to be in a sheltered position.

31

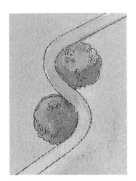

Figure 1

Figure 2

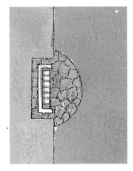

Figure 3

Right: The owners of this small town garden have opted for a formal layout with a high degree of symmetry emphasized by potted plants.

Far above right: This garden has a simple ground plan based on a cross. The rigid lines of the gravel paths are softened with herbaceous plants such as catmint, pinks and herbs.

BORDER DESIGN

This is very much related to the style of garden and whether you want a formal or informal feel. If the plot is irregular or the ground uneven, then broad sweeping curves would work well. You might also go for this if the garden is in a rural setting or if you want to create a wild or woodland area. Keep curves long and gentle. A scalloped edge will just compete with the form and texture of the flowers and foliage. Simple lines are restful and make mowing and edging easier.

In a long, narrow plot, the eye rapidly travels to the end, leaving the viewer with a sense of having seen everything at once. A simple solution to this problem is to use an S-shaped path (fig. 1). If the resultant staggered beds are planted to prevent a clear line of sight down the garden, you can create a real sense of mystery.

To make a garden feel intimate, make the paths narrow and the beds deep, and bring large plants close to the pathway at intervals so that you feel enveloped in flowers. This is an excellent way of dealing with a very small plot. If the eye is unable to see the boundary lines, it will assume the space is bigger than it really is.

Island beds are another possibility for informal gardens, but careful planning is needed to ensure that they blend in properly with the rest of the site. A small bed isolated within a large area of lawn usually looks out of scale. Plan the beds on paper, using flowing and interconnecting shapes that are pleasing to the eye.

In recent years there has been a tremendous resurgence of interest in formal garden design based on simple geometry of squares, rectangles and circles. You don't need an historic house to employ this approach. Formality works just as well in contemporary landscapes with modern architecture.

One of the classic formal layouts is the double border separated by a central pathway (fig. 2). This allows the opportunity to create a focal point at one or both ends of the axis. To add interest in a long, straight border, you could build a climber-covered pergola along the path or add alcoves to highlight some kind of ornament, a piece of topiary perhaps or a bench seat (fig. 3). Alternatively, you could cut out a square or circular area half way down the path, and center it with a feature such as a formal pool, tree, sculpture or bird bath (fig. 4).

A long, thin plot can be divided up into a number of smaller garden "rooms" with each plot given its own treatment and character (fig. 5). You might, for example, create a circular paved area at the center of one room with borders around the perimeter or you could divide the plot into four equal segments using crossing paths, edging the borders with a low clipped hedge to emphasize the formality.

For a modern feel, one design option is to divide the plot into two sections diagonally using a smooth curve. This dynamic line leads the eye right to the end of the border. It is important to give the viewer something worthwhile to focus on at the end such as a piece of sculpture. In a front garden you might use a line to emphasize the

Figure 4

USING A PLAN

A great way of planning a garden, or even just an individual border, is to create a plan on paper to allow you to better visualize the outcome. Once you have measured up the area to be planted, and mapped the position of existing features, you can transfer this information to squared paper. Devise a scale that allows as large a drawing as possible on the sheet so that you have plenty of room to mark in details like plant names and individual paving units. Next sketch in the shape of the new borders, or if working with an existing space, begin to mark down how the new plants will be arranged. Make sure you allow room for the plant's eventual size. The easiest way to do that is to mark each plant with a circle whose diameter corresponds to the plant's predicted spread.

Once you are happy with your plan, use it as your guide to mark out the position of the borders on the ground. A hose is a convenient way to mark out curving edges because it creates gentle curves, stays in position on its own and can be moved around easily. You will need to knock in small wooden stakes along your planned edges once you're satisfied, however, so that you have a permanent record of the plan.

Create circles by pushing in a metal pin with a string line attached that equates to the radius you want. Keep the line stretched taught as you move round the stake, marking the circle with pegs as you go.

When you have transferred your paper plan to the ground, it often helps to check the layout from an upstairs window before making any permanent changes.

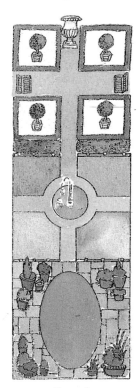

Figure 5

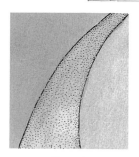

Figure 6

main entrance (fig. 6). You can also slow the speed at which the eye travels along the curve by punctuating the line with taller plants.

Yet another approach, useful for dealing with irregularly-shaped plots, is to mark out a series of interlocking circles or rectangles of different sizes that run through the central area (fig. 7). This creates an interesting open space in the center with flower borders flowing round the sides.

Figure 7

The non-planted area of a garden doesn't have to be lawn: it could be gravel, cobbles, paving, decking or the smooth reflective surface of water. The textural contrast enhances the effectiveness of the planting. And having a broad, open area also makes the garden feel more spacious.

Successful garden design is all about balance and proportion. It's important to consider three-dimensional space as well as the pattern on the ground. For example, a border may seem wide before planting, but when tall plants grow up they could make the bed seem narrow. Generally speaking, the bed should be at least as wide as the tallest element, with the exclusion of trees and house walls. Overly narrow borders not only look mean, but also don't allow as much scope for creative planting. If you are worried about having access, lay a stepping stone path through the middle from which to work.

GROUND PREPARATION

When you are ready to dig the borders, lift off the turf if necessary or kill the grass using a systemic herbicide such as Roundup. Then simply dig the dead roots and foliage back into the soil. Dig over the ground to a spade's depth, breaking up any large chunks. On badly-compacted ground you may need to double dig to ensure good drainage and root penetration. Never dig too deeply or you risk bringing up inferior subsoil from below the fertile level. You can spot this on some soils because the texture and color changes. For example, subsoil in heavy clay is orangey-yellow or blue-grey in color.

Remove any weeds and keep a look out for the roots of perennial weeds. These are usually quite fleshy. Dispose of them—not on the compost heap.

On poor soil, such as free-draining sand, apply a slow-release fertilizer in spring, raking it in according to the manufacturer's instructions. Do not overfeed as this causes soft growth that is vulnerable to pests and diseases, as well as to wind in exposed sites.

DIFFICULT SOILS

Sand Very light, sandy, free-draining soil requires plenty of well-rotted but bulky organic matter to be added, to keep it fertile and retain moisture. In high rainfall areas, these soils tend to be quite poor because there is nothing to trap the nutrients and stop them being washed away. It's best to apply organic matter as a thick surface mulch in late winter or early spring when the ground is still damp, so that the moisture is sealed in.

Clay These soils are inherently fertile, but are notoriously hard to cultivate. In areas where the ground is not frozen, they are too wet to work from fall until spring, while in summer, they are almost impenetrable when baked by the sun. Working the soil when too wet or too dry just destroys the crumb structure, making drainage an even bigger problem. During a wet winter, plant roots are liable to rot because the air spaces are filled with water and the roots drown. Digging in bulky organic matter is the key to taming clay soil. It causes the minute clay particles to clump together, leaving spaces for air and moisture between. This enables earthworms to colonize and break up the soil further. You can

also dig in grit to improve drainage or, alternatively, heap the soil up in the borders to give a domed profile. This helps to keep plant roots above the water table. Once you have begun to improve the drainage and organic content of clay, it becomes workable and easier to manage.

Peat This has a high organic content but can be poor in nutrients and sour, which means it is too acidic for plants other than heathland or certain woodland varieties. It can be "sweetened" with lime, but it's often better to stick to plants that really thrive in these conditions. There are nurseries that specialize in such plants.

CHOOSING AND BUYING PLANTS

There are many ways to buy perennials. You'll find a range at garden centers at the start of the season, usually in small pots. Later on in the season, you can buy plants in full leaf and even flower. These specimens come in larger pots and are more expensive, but are useful for filling gaps in an existing border. You can experiment with different groupings of them to make sure you're happy with the combination before purchase. It's a good idea when selecting plants to take a pocket guide to check descriptions and cultivation details, as information on the labels can be very sketchy.

Specialist nurseries stock a much wider range than garden centers and you can often get good advice about choosing plants to suit your particular conditions. Some places also have display gardens with lots of ideas for good combinations so take a notebook.

1. On new ground that has not recently been cultivated, especially soil that has been compacted, dig over with a spade, breaking up any large clods of soil.

2. Heavy soils benefit from the addition of well-rotted organic matter. Fork in generous quantities. The addition of coarse material such as chipped bark or gravel also helps with winter drainage.

3. On naturally poor or impoverished soils, apply a top dressing of slow-release fertilizer at the beginning of the season, being sure to follow the manufacturer's instructions.

PERENNIALS FROM SEED

Many people who live in remote areas far away from garden centers grow their perennials from seed. All that is needed is a cold frame to protect the sprouted seedlings in their pots and a small nursery bed where the plants can be grown on until they are large enough to go into the garden some two or three years later. This can be a good way to develop a perennial bed as it allows plenty of time to properly select a site and prepare the soil by incorporating a lot of organic material if necessary. An added bonus is that when the plants first bloom in the nursery bed, you can note the color and bloom time. This will enable you to site plants next to their perfect mates and create wonderful, eye-catching color combinations.

If you live too far away from a good nursery or garden center, or you are looking for more unusual varieties, you'll need to buy by mail order. It's difficult to know what the quality will be like in advance, so deal only with reputable companies and read the terms and conditions before ordering. The good companies are willing to

either pot up or plant out immediately, depending on the weather. Another advantage to buying mail order is that it is sometimes less expensive, especially when buying multiples of the same plant.

Whenever possible when buying ground cover plants, choose pot-bound plants that can be split into

give you an exchange or refund if you are not satisfied. It's worth paying a little more for the plants knowing you have a no-questions-asked guarantee behind each plant.

To save on the cost of postage, many plants are shipped bare-root, and the plants tend to be small. These are quite vulnerable and need prompt attention on arrival. Water well and

chunks with a knife, giving you more plants than you paid for. However, not all pot-bound plants are a good bargain if the roots are constricted, damaging the health of the plant.

Also, to get more value when buying plants that can easily be divided, choose those that have multiple crowns to allow you to divide the plant straight away to give several smaller plants.

IMPROVING AN EXISTING BORDER

You may find, even after good planning, that the border is less than satisfactory at certain times of year. Perhaps it lacks color some months, maybe there are gaps or perhaps some plants have not done as well as expected. You may also feel that the border lacks contrast in form or that the color scheme needs attention. Keep a note during the year of any necessary changes and perhaps even mark out the position of new or replacement plants with plastic labels or canes. You can then make up your order for a particular nursery in one go and either plant in fall or spring depending on conditions and availability.

PLANTING

Avoid planting in frosty weather or when the ground is very dry unless you are able to irrigate. Soak the plants thoroughly in a bucket of water, submerging them and waiting until the stream of air bubbles has stopped. Set the plants out at the correct distance. Dig each planting hole wider than the rootball but not so deep that you risk burying the crown. Some herbaceous perennials, such as heuchera, lady's mantle and certain grasses, have a habit of growing out of the ground and benefit from deeper planting. Normally though, set the level at the original planting depth. Don't be tempted to dig a hole that's only just big enough to drop the plant into, without first digging or forking over the area around the planting hole. On heavy soils, in particular, the roots will have difficulty growing out into the surrounding soil and growth

Left: Group together the plants before you buy to see whether the different colors and shapes complement each other.

1. No matter how moist the compost looks, always water before planting, by plunging the pot into a bucket of water.

2. Once planted, it is essential that perennials are watered in thoroughly to settle the soil closely around the roots.

3. Mulch the soil surface with organic matter to a depth of 4 inches to conserve moisture.

DIRECTORY OF FLOWER SHAPES

Bowls

*Paeonia, Papaver, Romneya,
Anemone, Geranium, Helleborus,
Malva, Oenothera*

Butterflies

Alstroemeria, Dictamnus, Gaura

Clouds

*Crambe cordifolia, Thalictrum delavayi,
Gypsophila, Alchemilla, Calamintha,
Brunnera, Epimedium, Heuchera*

Cones, domes and thimbles

*Centranthus, Allium spaerocephalon,
Eryngium*

Daisies

*Anthemis, Coreopsis, Doronicum,
Echinacea, Erigeron, Inula, Aster,
Rudbeckia, Leucanthemum,
Rhodanthemum*

Flat Plates and Umbrellas

*Achillea, Angelica, Sedum,
Foeniculum, Chaerophyllum*

Globes

*Agapanthus, Allium,
Armeria, Echinops*

Pincushions and posies

Knautia, Scabiosa, Astrantia

Plumes

*Astilbe, Macleaya, Rodgersia
pinnata, Aruncus*

Sculptures

Iris, Zantedeschia

Spikes and Pokers

*Lysimachia, Ajuga reptans, Cimicifuga,
Veronicastrum, Diascia rigescens,
Kniphofia, Linaria, Liriope, Lythrum,
Persicaria, Perovskia, Salvia, Liatris,
Stachys, Veratrum, Verbascum*

Tapering Spires

*Digitalis, Acanthus, Aconitum,
Delphinium, Lupinus, Ligularia 'The Rocket'*

Trumpets and Funnels

Crocosmia, Hemerocallis, Hosta, Lilium

Tubes and Bells

*Penstemon, Campanula, Bergenia,
Dierama, Nectaroscordum, Platycodon,
Pulmonaria, Symphytum*

Whorls

*Monarda, Phlomis, Ballota, Lamium,
Salvia verticillata*

Right: The very large, sculptural blooms of an *Iris ensata* cultivar.

Far right: Echinacea purpurea has daisy-like flowers with large cone-like centers.

Above right: The flowers of *Monarda* 'Adam' are shaggy, scarlet whorls.

Above far right: Kniphofia flowers form upright pokers, making a bold statement in the border.

1. One of the simplest methods of working out the relative positions of plants in a **border** is to arrange them in their pots on the prepared soil.

2. If you want to check your planting plan works before ordering the plants, use colored plant tags to represent the positions of different plants. This will help you visualize your scheme.

3. Another method is to create a three-dimensional version using canes of different lengths to represent the flowering heights. It's easy to spot where there may be problems and make any necessary adjustments.

Right: This tiered display of border phlox, deep blue monkshood, golden yellow *Inula* and plume poppy, is all the more eye-catching against a backdrop of clipped yew.

will be poor. Another mistake is to fill the hole with peat or compost. This acts like a sponge in winter, drawing moisture from surrounding earth and keeping the plant's roots saturated and vulnerable to rotting.

Instead, soak the base of the hole with water, put the plant in place and back-fill with good soil. Firm in with hands or a foot but avoid compacting the soil too much. Water in well.

Mulching with shredded or chipped bark, cocoa shells or gravel will help conserve moisture and is a good way to cut down on weeding.

PLANTING IN GROUPS

Herbaceous plants create the greatest impact when planted in large clumps or swathes of the same variety. They are best grouped in threes, fives, sevens and so on depending on the size of plant and area to be covered. It's very difficult to arrange an even number in a natural-looking way. This multiple planting can be expensive. Some plants can be raised cheaply from seed, but sowing is not an option for named cultivars because they don't come true.

Another alternative to save money on plants is to buy just a few and grow them on until the crown is large enough to be divided. Certain of the cranesbills, such as *Geranium* x *riversleaianum* 'Russell Prichard', are so vigorous that you'll only need to buy one plant to fill a space in the border. Stem and root cuttings can also be taken to build up stocks. See page 91 for details of propagation techniques.

Specimen perennials, such as goat's beard, *Aruncus dioicus*, and *Euphorbia characias wulfenii*, are normally planted singly unless the site is large.

BACKDROPS

To show off the flowers and foliage of herbaceous perennials to advantage, they need an appropriate background, usually one that provides contrast in terms of color and texture. This might mean setting a grouping against a large shrub or wall-trained climber. Plain brick walls and neatly-clipped hedges also make ideal backdrops because they are smooth and relatively featureless. Trellis panel screens also work well, especially when stained or painted to enhance the planting. Whatever you choose, try to keep the background uncluttered to throw the emphasis on to the plants.

Pale flowers can be used to dramatic effect against a dark evergreen hedge like yew. Conversely, try setting dark rich colors against a paler backdrop such as a weathered wooden fence, a pale stone wall or painted treillage.

Utilize walls, fences and trellis panels for training climbers and shrubs such as rose, clematis, ivy and so on.

DESIGNING WITH PERENNIALS

For a border to have a strong visual impact, it's vital to consider the habit of each plant and the shape and texture of the leaves and flowers. This is as important as color when combining plants. Flowers come in an infinite variety from simple daisies to curious designs like the toad lily (*Tricyrtis*). Some are fragrant and attractive to bees and butterflies. A few open only at dusk and are pollinated by night-flying insects, while others only stay out when the sun is shining, but close when it gets cloudy. The more time you spend looking at the structure of flowers and the insect life that visits them, the more remarkable they seem

to be. But when it comes to combining flowers in the border, you need to stand back and get an overview, first concentrating on form. Otherwise, it's easy to be seduced by color and give it too much priority when it comes to devising a planting plan. Play around on paper or with potted plants in the garden center or nursery, contrasting fluffy plumes with stiff daisy heads,

and spikes with flat plates. Arrange bowl-shaped flowers to emerge from a cloud of frothy bloom and try globes with trumpets. Visit open gardens whenever you can and keep a pen and notebook or camera handy to record combinations that really work well. Remember, adjacent plants need to be flowering at roughly the same time otherwise you lose the effect. Some

years a combination will work better than others, but part of the magic of gardening is that nothing is predictable.

In design terms, the purpose of foliage is not simply to act as a foil for flowers. It can also be a feature in its own right and a border containing foliage plants with contrasting leaf shapes, textures and colors can be just as exciting as one full of blooms.

Another point to remember when selecting perennial plants is that the leaves are far more enduring than the flowers, so you should always check out the foliage before buying. Plants like aconites and daylilies, whose newly-emerged foliage is particularly attractive, are well worth having, as are ones with foliage that develops good fall tints like some of the hardy geraniums and rodgersias.

Look out for the evergreens as well, including blue-leaved fescues, black ophiopogon, orange libertia, hellebores, bergenias, and some of the silver-leaved artemisias. As well as differences in color, leaves also have certain textural qualities which add interest both visually and on a tactile level. A good example is felting, which is usually silver or grey due to it's light-reflecting qualities, as seen in stachys, verbascum, *Salvia argentea* and *Lychnis coronaria*. Some leaves have a glaucous or waxy bloom, typically encountered in succulent and drought-resistant plants, such as many of the sedums, and grasses. In contrast there are leaves with a high gloss such as bergenia and acanthus as well as ones that are puckered; veratrums and hostas are good examples. Finally, don't forget that some plants are aromatic, releasing their scent when the leaves are disturbed by a passer-by or crushed between thumb and forefinger.

Above left: This late spring border looks fresh and lush and demostrates the beauty and importance of foliage, with hostas and grasses, silver stachys and lady's mantle.

Right: In a shady corner, *Fatsia japonica* makes a strong composition with hostas and ferns.

DIRECTORY OF FOLIAGE SHAPES

Small, rounded
Lysimachia nummularia, Ajuga, Alchemilla, Lychnis coronaria, Ballota

Large, broad or rounded
Darmera, Bergenia, Hosta, Astilboides, Veratrum

Needle-like
Foeniculum, Artemisia 'Powis Castle', Aster ericoides, Coreopsis verticillata

Ferny or lacy
Astilbe, Chaerophyllum, Acaena, Dicentra, Achillea, Artemisia stelleriana, ferns

Grassy
Armeria, dwarf Hemerocallis, Crocosmia, Kniphofia, Liatris, Libertia, Liriope, Ophiopogon, Carex

Arching, strap-shaped
Agapanthus, Iris, Hemerocallis, larger Kniphofia

Stiff, sword-shaped
Sisyrinchium, Iris (tall bearded and I. pallida), Crocosmia

Dramatic, jagged
Acanthus, Echinops, Angelica, Rheum, Crambe maritima, Cynara cardunculus, Rodgersia podophylla

Elegantly lobed .
Aconitum, Ligularia 'The Rocket', Anemone, Geranium, Astrantia, Macleaya, Malva moschata

Arrow-shaped
Arum, Persicaria amplexicaulis, Zantedeschia

Heart-shaped
Hosta, Epimedium, Brunnera, Doronicum, Houttuynia, Viola

PLANTS WITH SCULPTURAL QUALITIES

Acanthus spinosus

Agapanthus

Allium

Angelica archangelica

Bergenia purpurascens

Carex elata 'Aurea'

Crocosmia 'Lucifer'

Cynara cardunculus

Darmera peltata

Dierama pulcherrimum

Echinops bannaticus 'Taplow Blue'

Eryngium, large-flowered types

Euphorbia characias wulfenii

Hemerocallis, tall cultivars

Hosta

Iris, tall bearded

Iris pallida

Kniphofia, large-flowered cultivars

Macleaya cordata

Matteuccia struthiopteris

Miscanthus sinensis

Paeonia lactiflora

Persicaria bistorta 'Superba'

Phlomis

Rheum palmatum

Rodgersia

Sedum 'Herbstfreude' (syn. 'Autumn Joy')

Sisyrinchium striatum

Veratrum nigrum

Verbascum

Zantedeschia aethiopica

SCULPTURAL ELEMENTS

Some perennials have a well-defined outline and act like living sculptures. You can generate a very modern or subtropical look by incorporating a large proportion of them in the same border along with sword-shaped foliage plants, such as yuccas and phormiums, or ones with very large leaves, such as *Fatsia japonica* (false castor oil plant) and *Rhus typhina* (sumac). Sculptural plants work well adjacent to the house, echoing the strong lines and solidity of the building. Like bright colors, they are attention-grabbing and can have a marked effect on perspective. Used further down the border they can foreshorten

Left: The stiff, upright leaves and poker-like flowers of *Kniphofia* 'Shining Sceptre' give it a sculptural quality and make it stand out from the surrounding foliage.

Above: Miscanthus are statuesque plants, ideal as focal points. The narrow foliage contrasts with the surrounding *Geranium psilostemon* and alchemilla.

CONTRASTING UPRIGHTS AND HORIZONTALS

the view because the eye assumes that large, well-defined objects must be relatively close. By planting taller architectural specimens among plants of more diffuse character, you can make a bold statement, adding drama and visual excitement to the garden. Use sparingly, however, as the eye soon becomes tired of contrast.

Some plants, such as iris, kniphofia, hemerocallis, sisyrinchium, verbascum, and veronicastrum, have a strongly upright feel with many parallel stems and flower heads. Many grasses also fall into this category, particularly some of the lovely forms of miscanthus.

If you combine and contrast plants like these with ones which have a broadly horizontal profile (such as sedum, achillea, geranium, alchemilla and also any plants that are used in multiple groupings to make low spreading masses, or front-of-the-border ground cover plants), the results can be very eye-catching indeed.

41

Above: Catmint (*Nepeta*) is a lovely long-flowered filler for a sunny, well-drained position. Here it is used to edge a pastel border of *Sisyrinchium striatum* 'Aunt May' with pink and white annual cosmos.

Right: Variegated apple mint (*Mentha suaveolens* 'Variegata') weaves its way through a border of *Penstemon* 'Ruby' and *Nepeta prattii*, lifting the darker colors.

FILIGREE FILLERS AND FOILS

Plants with airy, diaphanous flowers or feathery, wispy foliage are essential for filling in gaps in the border and for use as foils for more substantial blooms and leaves. In particular, this category includes plants with very soft, even neutral, coloring exemplified by the green of ballota, lady's mantle and euphorbia. Cool-colored plants which have mauve, steel-blue, silver or gray coloring also work well as a foil for flowers at the warm end of the spectrum – yellows, oranges, reds and pinks. Some examples of filigree foils at work include bush roses underplanted with catmint; the pretty annual blue love-in-a-mist (*Nigella*) with tall bearded iris, and silver *Artemisia* 'Powis Castle' combined with pink penstemons. A border planted entirely with these kinds of plants would lack any feeling of substance. Generally these fuzzy-focus plants must be mixed with more well-defined, even sculptural forms, to be successful.

Diaphanous plants soften the look of a border and if a relatively large proportion is used, can create a romantic, even dream-like quality. This is especially true when taller, "see-through" kinds, such as airy grasses, fennel, and *Verbena bonariensis*, are woven in between plants of a more substantial nature.

Taking things a step further, if you want to create the illusion of distance and make the garden seem longer than it is, plant an increasingly high proportion of filigree plants as you move toward the end of the border. You can increase the illusion if you concentrate on the recessive colors like gentle blues, grays and mauves.

STAGGERED DISPLAYS (AND BREAKING THE RULES)

Broadly speaking, the taller plants go at the back of the border and progressively shorter ones toward the front. This arrangement helps hide the bare and often unsightly bases of taller perennials. But if you are too regimented in the way that you place your plants, you'll end up with a very stiff, uninspiring display. Try to create some kind of rhythm running through the planting, an undulating motion of peaks and troughs, as well as a seasonal rhythm with groups of plants that flower together gradually giving way to others. Don't confine all your tall sculptural specimens to the rear just because of their height. Bring one or two forward among a sea of low-growing plants and give them the space to shine just like you would any other work of art. Break up the edges too, and allow plants to spill out over paving and, yes, even lawn. Some plants are wonderfully exuberant and need room for expression. They can be clipped back at the end of the season and the lawn will recover.

Taller plants of substance work well as edge breakers. Try agapanthus, hemerocallis, bearded iris and verbascum. Plants like these give the eye something to focus on as it travels along the border and the more skillful you are at catching the eye in this way, the larger and more interesting the garden appears to be.

Toward the front of the border you may need to plan carefully to fill gaps left when early-flowering perennials like oriental poppies (*Papaver orientale*) and bleeding heart (*Dicentra spectabilis*) die away to nothing.

We've all planted something in the wrong spot, and it's frustrating when you inadvertently obliterate another plant growing behind. Happily you can move most perennial plants around with impunity.

WEAVERS AND SEEDERS

Plants with a wandering habit are often despised as weeds, but there are those that "travel" in an inoffensive manner, including foliage plants such as the variegated apple and ginger mints and grey-white *Artemisia ludoviciana*, as well as the Japanese anemones and Californian tree poppy. Above-ground spreaders include *Lysimachia nummularia* (creeping Jenny), *Ajuga reptans* (carpet bugleweed) and many hardy geraniums. If you add self-seeders, you end up with a degree of uncertainty as to how things are going to turn out. True, some plants do have to be grubbed out or cut back, but once you relax a little and let plants interact in a more natural way, you'll be amazed at some of the wonderful combinations that occur. Also be prepared to have seedlings cropping up some distance from the original plant, taken by the wind or by birds – they usually thrive best where they've put themselves.

As well as the hardy annuals and biennials, such as nasturtium, opium poppy, foxglove, California poppy (*Eschscholzia*), love-in-a-mist, and calendula, many perennials can be relied upon to self-sow without assistance, including those in the list (right). However, be careful next to gravel or paving without mortar as this is difficult ground to manage by hand without resorting to weed killer.

PLANTS WITH A FILIGREE TEXTURE OR NEUTRAL COLOR

Alchemilla mollis
Artemisia, finely-cut foliage types
Aster ericoides
Aster lateriflorus 'Horizontalis'
Aster turbinellus
Ballota
Calamintha
Chaerophyllum hirsutum 'Roseum'
Deschampsia caespitosa
Erigeron karvinskianus
Eryngium tripartitum
Foeniculum vulgare 'Purpureum'
Gaura lindheimeri
Heuchera
Lysimachia ephemerum
Nepeta x faassenii
Origanum laevigatum 'Herrenhausen'
Origanum vulgare
Perovskia 'Blue Spire'
Stipa gigantea
Verbena bonariensis

SEEDERS

Alchemilla mollis
Angelica archangelica
Aquilegia
Campanula latiloba
Campanula persicifolia
Centaurea montana
Centranthus ruber
Erigeron karvinskianus
Euphorbia dulcis 'Chameleon'
Foeniculum vulgare 'Purpureum'
Hesperis matronalis
Lychnis coronaria
Meconopsis cambrica
Verbascum olympicum
Viola labradorica

Color has the power to move us in an emotional way and is one of the most important elements in enhancing the sensual experience of gardening. By careful manipulation of color we can create different moods and effects within the garden – calming and soothing or exciting and stimulating, for example. Sensitive use of color has a marked effect on the success of any planting scheme. There are guidelines as to which colors work well together, but some of the most interesting effects come from breaking the rules. At the end of the day, color scheming is a matter for personal taste.

In recent years there has been a huge increase in interest in interior design. People are becoming a lot more adventurous with color in their homes and the willingness to experiment has spilled out into the garden. You can buy a host of outdoor furniture, fabrics, tableware, floor tiles, containers and lighting in a wide selction of colors and designs as well as an amazing choice of wood dyes, paints and masonry finishes. So where do plants fit in to the scheme of things? In terms of color, they are quite simply part of the palette as they come in an infinite number of shades and can be used almost like paint on a canvas. This is not a new idea; the English Arts and Crafts garden designer Gertrude Jekyll was well known for taking this approach, and at in his garden at Giverny in France, artist Claude Monet created the most sumptuous stage sets.

Flowering and foliage perennials form the basis of any color scheme during the summer months. The range is enormous, but even with

careful planning, there will be gaps when few plants are actually blooming or periods when the scheme needs strengthening in some way. This is where annuals and tender perennials and, to a lesser extent, bulbs, come in useful. They are the perfect tools for adding small or large patches of color to strengthen a scheme. Color scheming is much harder to maintain between late fall and early spring, and is often abandoned or allowed to slide for lack of plant material.

As with interior decorating, deciding on a color theme for your garden or for a specific area within the garden usually depends on a mixture of things, principally your personal preferences and the mood or flavor you want to create. You may also be inspired by existing features such as the colors in paving or a brick wall, the flowers of an established climber, or the color of distant hills. It's useful to get together color swatches, photographs and plant lists before embarking on any major garden projects, but planning can only take you so far in gardening since plants have a habit of not behaving as anticipated. You really have to compare the colors of two plants in situ to tell whether they work together. But then that's what makes the whole process so exciting.

painting with perennials

Once the framework of a garden is firmly established, you can begin to overlay it with colors and textures in the form of plants. There's a bewildering array of shades to experiment with, but skillful and restrained use of color is the key to success.

Far left: A modern color scheme featuring lime green euphorbia, silver-grey ballota, bronze fennel, black-purple iris and *Lysimachia ciliata* 'Firecracker'. Red and salmon-buff flowers add some vibrancy.

Figure 1

CONTRASTING AND HARMONIZING COLORS

The color wheel (fig. 1) is a useful device for working out the details of a garden color scheme. If you want to create a harmonious picture, combine colors that are adjacent to one another on the wheel or which contain the same colors, such as red and purple or green and blue. For a much more dramatic effect, combine colors that are opposite each other on the wheel such as yellow and purple or blue and orange. These are known as complementary or contrasting colors and create vivid schemes when combined.

MONOCHROME BORDERS

These can be extremely stylish and are favored by people with a minimalist approach to decoration who follow the maxim, "less is more." But, with the exception of white and yellow, it can be difficult to maintain such a restricted palette through the year unless you are prepared to fill in the gaps with temporary plants, and this can mean extra work. It is often more successful to link the planting with a permanent feature such as painted furniture, treillage, fences, decking or containers, either in harmonizing or contrasting colors. That way you'll always have a strong color focus regardless of whether or not the plants are in flower.

Top: The color wheel is used to assess how well colors combine together.

Above: A gentle scheme of soft greys and white, using foliage as well as flowers to add color.

Right: A white garden with *Crambe cordifolia*, astrantia and campanulas.

Far right: Silvery cardoon and artemisia mingle with blue-grey hostas and white marguerites.

Far top right: White-variegated dogwood (*Cornus*) forms a good backdrop to apple mint foliage and white phlox.

WHITE

A classic example of monochrome scheming is the white garden. In the West, white symbolizes purity, innocence and peace. It is also a color of spiritual significance.

White is the most dominant color in the garden and in strong sunlight it can be almost too bright unless diluted with greens, greys and silvers. But you can use this visibility to your advantage in shade, where white flowers and foliage create a cool, tranquil atmosphere. White flowers positively glow in twilight or under a full moon, and a white garden can be transformed at night with carefully-arranged lighting. The white garden is the easiest of all to create and to maintain throughout the year because the choice of plants is so great. White gardens incorporate every shade of green foliage as well as silver and grey. They include all the white-variegated plants and a myriad of white flowers. Perennial species often have a white-flowered version, and white is a very common flower color in nature. Pale blue associates well with the white garden, emphasizing the peace and calm.

Far left: Hostas 'Halcyon' and 'Frances Williams' add a cool blue tone among blue geranium and violas.

Above left: The crisp, silver stems of *Perovskia* 'Blue Spire' set off the blue flowers.

Below left: The striking honeywort, *Cerinthe major* 'Purpurascens' has an overall blue cast and navy blue-tinged flower bracts.

Above: The spiny blooms of the sea holly, *Eryngium* x *zabelii*, are a beautiful shade of lavender-blue.

Above right: *Brunnera macrophylla* is a useful blue-flowered perennial for shady sites.

BLUE

Any single color scheme can become rather monotonous if overdone. All-blue schemes are particularly difficult and can end up looking rather dull and dreary. It can be a mistake to doggedly stick to a particular shade. A sprinkling of a harmonizing or complementary color, for example, has the effect of enhancing and intensifying the core color. This need not be done purely with plants. You might achieve a satisfactory balance in the garden simply by planting a blue border against an orange-red brick wall, or by placing large terra-cotta pots within the bed. To add sparkle to an all-blue border, mix in a proportion of silver and lime green foliage and a smattering of white flowers or, as an alternative, use purple and bronze foliage and a few purple flowers, perhaps, with a dusting of silver foliage. Most blue flowers contain red to varying degrees so purple is a natural partner to blue.

Like green, blue has healing properties and light blue is a popular choice for hospital wards. Sky blue is believed to aid powers of communication and indigo blue to facilitate contemplation and introspection.

Blue is a cool, relaxing color and is associated with water and the sea. It can reduce the apparent temperature of a hot, sunny courtyard and in the relatively dull "blue" light of northern latitudes, you can get away with using quite vivid blues for walls, trellis and containers, reminiscent of Mediterranean climes.

Blues, greys, purples and mauves are receding colors and tend to make a space feel larger than it really is. Use them at the end of a garden that borders on to open countryside to help merge the boundary line.

YELLOW

Yellow represents clarity and is the sunshine color, second only to white in its ability to stand out in shade, where it produces the effect of dappled sunlight. But in full sunshine, when used skillfully, yellow is softer in its effect. Yellow is also a color strongly associated with spring.

There's no shortage of yellow flowers. You can select from hundreds of blooms in shades ranging from cream to deep gold, and there are plenty of perennials and shrubs with yellow and gold-variegated foliage, too. The only danger with schemes which use mainly yellow flowers and yellow-variegated foliage, is that the border can look tired, and even scorched, especially when situated in full sun.

But the addition of fresh, cooling greens and blue-tinged foliage plants remedies the situation and again, a sprinkling of purple or blue flowers will help make the yellow appear even more vibrant. For a very contemporary feel, try blue-painted trellis as a backdrop to the border, or place a blue bench or seat in the midst of the planting.

Top left: Golden elder makes the perfect backdrop for lupines.

Top center: The tall spikes of *Kniphofia* 'Wrexham Buttercup' make an eye-catching display.

Left: Touches of purple intensify the soft yellow blooms in this very full double border.

Above: The daylily, *Hemerocallis* 'Green Gold'.

Right: Alchemilla makes a cooling foil for evening primrose and mullein.

PINK

This is a relaxing and balancing color, helping to soothe and calm frayed nerves, especially when combined with green. Pink is strongly associated with love, and has had romantic connotations throughout history. It is also very much a color of early summer and of childhood.

There is a wide range of pinks. The coolest are the blue-pinks: mauve-, lilac- and cerise-pink. These colors work well with silver and purple foliage, touches of crimson-red, and rich purple. Generally speaking, blue-pinks do not sit well with orange or strong yellow or indeed with yellow-pinks, such as salmon, apricot and peach. But these colors, along with clear pinks (pure red diluted with white), can work well with clear yellow, creating a bright, fresh and cheerful effect.

Pink is quite a visible color in shade and at twilight, and the blue-pinks work particularly well in cloudier northern climes. In hot sun they can seem a little dull and flat.

PINK BUTTERFLIES

Gaura lindheimeri 'Siskiyou Pink' is an absolute must for any plant enthusiast's garden. Of course, Gaura lindheimeri has been around for a long while and is invaluable for its long blooming season, but 'Siskiyou Pink' adds another dimension with its deep rose-pink flowers dancing on waving stems like butterflies. Like its cousin, it is drought tolerant and a good candidate for waterwise gardening.

Far left: A traditional herbaceous border in shades of pink, featuring old-fashioned *Galega* 'His Majesty', *Achillea millefolium* 'Lilac Beauty' and silvery lamb's ears (*Stachys byzantina*).

Center: The beautiful blooms of peony 'Sarah Bernhardt'.

Left: A romantic purple-pink scheme of opium poppies, foxgloves, *Geranium psilostemon* and roses.

Below left: Fleshy blue-green leaves of sedum are the perfect foil for *Geranium* x *oxonianum*.

Below: The dish-shaped blooms of the evening primrose *Oenothera speciosa* 'Siskiyou'.

PURPLE

This is very much the color of the New Age and spirituality. The various shades of purple are believed to facilitate perception and enlightenment, contemplation, the release of potential and universal understanding. Purple would be ideal for a garden designed for meditation.

Purple is an easier color than blue to work with in the garden because there are many more plants to choose from in a much wider palette. Purple is a much warmer color than blue because of the red element.

Shades of purple vary from the palest lilac-pink to dramatic black-purples and also includes glowing purple-reds and magenta, as well as lilacs and lavender on the blue side. As well as flowers, there are many foliage plants with purple or bronze-tinged leaves and others with black-purple coloring. To freshen an all-purple scheme in a subtle way, use pale apple and lime green as well as silver and grey foliage. And to make a purple scheme richer, add "cool" reds like cerise and crimson.

Right: Verbena corymbosa has soft lilac blooms. The plants weave around in the border, forming airy clouds of flowers among the other plants.

Above right: A froth of aromatic catmint (*Nepeta* x *faassenii*) spills over a gravel path.

Center: Iris ensata cultivars thrive in the damp soil of a bog garden.

Far right: Dark bronze fennel forms a backdrop for drumstick alliums and French lavender in this moody scheme.

ORANGE AND RED

These are energetic, happy, stimulating, rather than relaxing colors. And like yellow and white, oranges and reds are extremely eye catching. Both have connections with heat and sexuality. Orange is the color of fall and of burning. Red is traditionally associated with romantic love and in some cultures, with luck. In nature, red is often an indication of danger. It is also the most visible color for people with impaired sight.

There are blue-reds, true reds and orange-reds but in an all-red border, you can get away with using all three together provided there's plenty of rich or pale green foliage to act as a neutral foil. This would create a very vibrant scheme with tropical and exotic overtones.

But if you prefer something cooler and more relaxing, go for blue-reds: crimsons, black-reds and cerise, and

combine them with purple, bronze and silver-grey foliage plants and a smattering of purple flowers.

Orange ranges from clear citrus to rich earthy and metallic tones such as burnt umber, bronze, copper and brown. Depending on the setting, props or garden accents, and the plants that are chosen, all-orange schemes can evoke desert-like heat, tropical exuberance, or the gentle slide into fall. Hot flame colors like orange and scarlet work perfectly together, again with green foliage as a cooling foil. Bronze-brown leaves also enhance orange.

But be careful: too much bright red or orange in a garden in summer could be overwhelming especially in the relatively dull "blue" light of northern climes. In that situation, it's a good idea to set these bright schemes against cooler, more relaxing ones like blue and purple.

Above: Red and orange blooms combine perfectly with purple foliage.

Far left: Euphorbia griffithii 'Fireglow' intermingles with tender African daisies (*Arctotis*).

Center: A blue-grey bench makes the perfect focal point at the end of these "hot" borders.

Left: The blooms of the choice verbascum cultivar 'Helen Johnson' are an unusual blend of salmon and buff.

COLOR DYNAMICS

Except in cottage gardens, it's no longer fashionable to grow flowers in a jumble of different shades. The use of color tends to be more sophisticated nowadays, although quiet and bright schemes seem equally popular. If you want to use lots of different colors in the garden, you can do this quite subtly by visually separating different areas so that you walk from one scheme to the next, but don't see the whole picture at once. Another technique for use in a long border is to start with one color and gradually move towards a contrasting shade or simply make waves of darker and lighter shades within the same palette. You can also create quite a crescendo by surrounding bright, rich attention-grabbing colors with less eye-catching shades from the opposite side of the color wheel. Where two borders are separated by a lawn or another kind of open space you could set a cool border, for example one planted with blues, purples and silvers, opposite a hot border planted with red, orange and bronze. And since some color schemes are difficult to maintain at certain times of the year, you could plan a border that started out as one color scheme at the start of the season and went through subtle changes to arrive somewhere completely different by the fall.

DRAMATIC AND UNUSUAL SCHEMES

In recent years, experimentation with color scheming in gardens has led to some interesting combinations being thought up. Perennials with unusual, even strange, coloring are in vogue, including green and black-flowered plants, and these will often suggest an entire color scheme. Many new plants are being bred with these schemes in mind. Try the following combinations of colors for a very interesting and up-to-date approach.

Rich purples and deep blues mixed with velvet browns, burnt oranges and clear citrus flowers with foliage in various shades of green.

Maroon, plum, clear red and black flowers mixed with green, deep purple-black and red-tinged foliage.

Pale terra-cotta, biscuit and cream flowers mixed with blue and silver-grey foliage. Combine these colors with strong burnt orange and rich brown highlights.

Purple-black and other very deep purples with pale mauves and lilacs, lime green and silver-grey foliage.

Black and white flowers with blue-grey and silver foliage.

Left: This airy scheme of allium seedheads, viola, diascia and scabious has a distinctly romantic feel.

Above: An unusual mixture of colors with a contemporary feel: brown-maroon irises mix with sharp orange geum and aquilegias in pink, white and blue.

Right: Dramatic blacks – violas, *Ophiopogon planiscapus* 'Nigrescens' and tender *Aeonium* 'Zwartkop'.

BLACK OR NEARLY BLACK FLOWERS

This list also includes annuals, biennials and bulbs, as black flowers are few and far between.

Alcea rosea 'Nigra'

Aquilegia 'Magpie'

Aquilegia vulgaris 'William Guiness'

Centaurea 'Black Ball'

Cosmos atrosanguineus

Dianthus barbatus nigrescens 'Sooty'

Fritillaria persica 'Adiyaman'

Geranium phaeum

Hemerocallis 'Black Magic'

Iris 'Black as Night', 'Black Swan', and 'Superstition'

Iris chrysographes 'Black Knight'

Lilium 'Black Beauty', 'Black Dragon' and Black Magic Group

Monarda 'Mahogany'

Nemophila menzesii 'Penny Black'

Papaver orientale 'Black and White'

Papaver paeoniflorum 'Black Peony'

Sedum telephium maximum 'Atropurpureum'

Tulipa 'Queen of Night' and 'Black Parrot'

Veratrum nigrum

Viola 'Bowles' Black' and 'Mollie Sanderson'

PERIOD COLOR SCHEMES

Formal gardening is in fashion now as is the desire to evoke a period or historic feel, by choosing classic plants like peony, iris, and verbascum, and restrained color schemes. Herbs and wildflowers are also favored because they have been used for centuries and never look modern or overbred.

The white monochrome garden is a popular choice, and works well in a formal setting. A subtle arrangement is the silver and grey foliage scheme where flowers are kept to a narrow palette of white, pink and mauve. Equally subtle is the all-green scheme using green flowers, lime-green and yellow foliage and dark evergreens.

Plants with "heritage" colors such as dusky pinks, soft apricots, plum, velvet browns, watercolor blues and purples, are being used more and more and this has meant that as well as new introductions, old varieties of plants like tall bearded iris have come back into popular use. You'll also find many more soft-colored annuals in the seed catalogues.

59

Signs of spring can come long before the trees break into leaf. At first glance you might miss the green bulb shoots pushing up through the ground, but once you see one, you see another. If you have planned well, there will be whole carpets coming through along the edges of paths and driveways, next to the terrace or deck, surrounding your favorite specimen trees, in swathes in the lawn and in pockets between plants in the border. In the colder regions, cold spells and late snow flurries may temporarily halt their growth, but ultimately flower buds appear and the whole garden begins to come to life once more. Many gardeners don't use bulbs in borders because the dying foliage can mar later-flowering displays, but low-growing kinds fade away unobtrusively, and the emerging leaves of herbaceous perennials will camouflage them.

Of course some of the perennials are evergreen, and a few delight us with their early blooms. To do well, most need a protected site that is sheltered from searing winds. The canopy provided by trees can create a beneficial microclimate at ground level, and a space between evergreen shrubs or on the sunniest side of a hedge is also ideally suited for early plantings. In addition, the heat given out by heated buildings and sunny

early birds

Spring is an uplifting season, full of promise for the year ahead. Slowly but surely the garden comes to life, with early bulbs and resilient perennials making a brave show. But then, as the weather improves, there's a sudden explosion of fresh growth.

garden walls or paved areas can also make a surprising difference in temperature, ensuring the survival of some and advancing the flowering time of others. So many winter and spring-flowering plants are fragrant, and when grown in a sheltered spot, the perfume is captured and concentrated. If you have a narrow bed at

the base of a sunny wall, you could try the wonderfully-fragrant winter-flowering iris (*Iris unguicularis*) which has large lavender-blue flowers and evergreen foliage.

As the weeks go by, the foliage of summer-flowering perennials grows at an amazing rate. Groups of spring-flowering perennials and bulbs add splashes of color and the new growth, often subtly colored itself, makes the perfect foil. It's a good idea to concentrate the bulbs and perennials that only flower in spring in certain areas of the garden, especially those plants whose foliage has little to offer during the summer. Team such plants up with spring-flowering trees and shrubs for maximum impact.

Of course many of the perennials that begin flowering in May continue to bloom for months, sometimes continuously or else with a rest when simple pruning and a boost of feeding and watering can set them off again with renewed vigor. And plants that are grown chiefly for their foliage effect will of course endure through the season. It's exciting to see some of the dramatic leaves unfurl in spring, especially those with interesting spring tints, and then to watch the way they interact with flowering plants in the summer and fall garden.

Far left: This elegant blue and white scheme features white tulips and English daisies, variegated honesty (*Lunaria*), hostas, grasses and forget-me-nots (*Myosotis*).

EARLY SPRING INTEREST

So much depends on the weather and how sheltered the site is, but if you are lucky enough to be snow-free during early spring, it's worth introducing some very early-flowering perennials and bulbs. We all need a lift at this time of year and seeing fresh leaves and flowers lets us know that spring is just waiting in the wings. Many early-flowering plants are shade-tolerant woodlanders and can be used as ground cover under trees. If you have a group of reasonably tall trees, plant in naturalistic drifts under them and use a bark mulch or leafmold to cover any bare soil. Alternatively, mark out a path through the trees, edging it with clumps of bulbs such as the early dwarf golden daffodil 'February Gold' coming up through a band of red, purple or bronze-leaved barrenwort (*Epimedium*), or on a smaller scale, snowdrops with the ruby-red primrose 'Wanda'.

Early perennials and bulbs can also be used to liven up bare soil beneath roses or to underplant shrubs with colored bark such as the dogwoods (*Cornus*), willows (*Salix*) and some of the maples, such as *Acer palmatum* 'Sango-kaku'. Color scheming would strengthen the impact of a group. You could, for example, take the pink-flowered *Viburnum* x *bodnantense* and underplant with pink *Helleborus orientalis*, purple-leaved bergenia and clumps of the tall, large-flowered snowdrop 'S. Arnott'.

To provide shelter and an attractive background for early blooms, plant early-flowering perennials and bulbs in pockets between evergreen shrubs and conifers. A north-facing border backed by a brick wall softened with wall shrubs and climbers such as variegated ivies, camellias or *Garrya elliptica* 'James Roof', which has long, silver-grey catkins, would be ideal for a winter-interest scheme, since so many of the season's plants are shade tolerant. Here you could use some of the brightly-variegated plants that might look out of place in the wild garden. For a stylish green and white scheme, try the white-striped gladdon iris, *Lamium maculatum* 'White Nancy' and *Arum italicum italicum* 'Marmoratum' between low-growing shrubs like sarcococca and skimmia.

Left: The *Helleborus foetidus* 'Wester Flisk Group' has red stems which contrast with the apple green flowers.

Below: A pink primrose nestles among blue scillas in a woodland planting.

Right: Arum italicum italicum 'Marmoratum' has handsome foliage in early spring, followed by a sculptural white "spathe" and orange berries later in the year.

Some perennials take up a lot of space in summer, spreading out from a central point. Such plants include some of the cranesbills, like *Geranium* 'Ann Folkard', *Geranium riversleaianum* 'Russel Prichard' and 'Mavis Simpson', but in spring the ground around them is bare. Make use of this temporary space by planting sun-loving dwarf bulbs around the crowns of the plants. By the time the stems have grown out again, the bulb foliage will have died down discretely.

FOLIAGE PERENNIALS FOR EARLY SPRING

Arum italicum italicum 'Marmoratum'
Bergenia
Carex buchananii
Carex oshimensis 'Evergold'
Cortaderia selloana 'Aureolineata'
Epimedium
Iris foetidissima 'Variegata'
Lamium maculatum 'White Nancy'
Ophiopogon planiscapus 'Nigrescens'

FLOWERING PERENNIALS FOR EARLY SPRING

Helleborus argutifolius
Helleborus foetidus
Helleborus orientalis
Iris unguicularis
Primula 'Wanda'

EARLY SPRING BULBS

Anemone blanda
Crocus chrysanthus
Crocus x luteus 'Golden Yellow'
Crocus tommasinianus
Cyclamen coum
Eranthis hyemalis
Galanthus elwesii
Galanthus nivalis
Iris histrioides 'Major'
Iris reticulata
Leucojum vernum
Narcissus 'February Gold', 'Peeping Tom' and 'Tête à Tête'
Scilla bifolia
Scilla mischtschenkoana

FOLIAGE PERENNIALS FOR MIDSPRING

Ferns
Hemerocallis
Mentha suaveolens 'Variegata'
Milium effusum 'Aureum'
Paeonia

FLOWERING PERENNIALS FOR MIDSPRING

Bergenia
Brunnera macrophylla
Darmera peltata
Doronicum
Epimedium
Euphorbia amygdaloides robbiae
Euphorbia characias wulfenii
Euphorbia cyparissias
Euphorbia myrsinites
Euphorbia polychroma
Mertensia pulmonarioides
Pulmonaria
Symphytum
Trillium

BULBS FOR MIDSPRING

Anemone nemorosa
Chionodoxa
Convallaria majalis
Crocus
Erythronium
Hyacinthus orientalis
Leucojum aestivum
Muscari armeniacum
Narcissus
Ornithogalum nutans
Puschkinia scilloides
Scilla siberica
Tulipa

PLANTS FOR MIDSPRING

During midspring, the whole garden begins to come back to life with new leaves and blossoms sprouting on trees and shrubs; and herbaceous foliage, including ferns, breaking through the soil. Daylily (*Hemerocallis*) foliage is an eye-catching bright lime green and many peonies have striking red or purple new shoots. Make a feature of the new shoots by planting clumps of dwarf bulbs around them.

There's a greater choice of flowering perennials at this time of year, with euphorbias featuring strongly and daisy-like leopard's bane making a bold show. Counter the prevailing acid greens and yellows with blue, by planting carpets of blue-flowered bulbs such as chionodoxa, scilla, and muscari. These will multiply happily but to get these diminutive plants to put on a good show in the first year, plant in groups of at least 30 bulbs.

Right: Euphorbia amygdaloides robbiae creates a carpet of lime flowers in mid spring

Above: Dainty yellow *Viola glabella* makes a pretty combination with pink dog's tooth violet (*Erythronium*) in a woodland setting.

Right: Elephant's ears (*Bergenia*) makes a fine show in spring.

Dwarf early-flowering tulips, such as *Tulipa kaufmanniana* and *T. greigii*, are also useful for adding a splash of color among developing herbaceous plants. To create a semi-wild, natural-looking planting, try combining pockets of daffodils, wood anemones and erythroniums with ferns, *Brunnera macrophylla*, epimediums, silver-mottled pulmonarias, Virginia cowslip and ornamental comfrey. In a bog garden, you can enjoy the unfurling fronds of moisture-loving ferns like *Matteuccia*, *Onoclea* or *Osmunda*, and the curious flowers of *Darmera* that are later replaced by spherical leaves. Consider making a real feature of an existing spring-flowering shrub by planting a tiered display of perennials and bulbs beneath it and completing the picture with spring bedding plants. By summer, this area will have faded into the background but by then new parts of the garden will have taken over and come to the fore.

Plant in full view of the house so that you can look out at something fresh and cheerful. Some bergenia cultivars have excellent flowers at this time of year and with their glossy rounded foliage make good edging plants, strong enough to line a front drive, or to add early color along the front of a summer-flowering border.

LATE SPRING

This is the time when the garden bursts forth with flowers. Soft pastel shades take over from sharp primary colors and old-fashioned flowers, like peony and bearded iris, silver stachys, violas and violet-blue hardy geraniums, bloom alongside roses. This kind of planting would create a romantic feel for a garden and would be perfect in a period setting. In a sunny, well-drained border you could add a few sumptuous tissue-paper blooms of pink, white or plum-colored oriental poppies and frilly-petalled parrot tulips. The almost purple-black tulip 'Queen of Night' and tall, drumstick alliums in shades of pink and purple would also work well coming up through lower-growing plants.

For a lightly-shaded spot on deep, moisture-retentive soil you could create an all-white scheme with a lacecap viburnum as the main focus. Planting could include elegant white *Dicentra spectabilis* and *Aconitum* 'Ivorine' with a foreground of *Viola cornuta* 'Alba', *Lamium* 'White Nancy' and London pride (*Saxifraga* x *urbium*). To add foliage interest, use the fresh new leaves of white-variegated hostas and soft green lady's mantle.

By late spring and early summer, the bog garden is beginning to look very lush with moisture-loving ferns and sedges, hostas and ornamental rhubarb (*Rheum*). Flowering interest comes in the form of bistort (*Persicaria*), the exotic blooms of *Zantedeschia*, richly-colored Japanese water iris and *Iris sibirica*, and the orange-red bracts of *Euphorbia griffithii*.

Cottage gardens are at their best in late spring and early summer and fragrant plants abound, including sweet rocket, violas, catmint, early daylily species and lily-of-the-valley. Many of the old-fashioned annuals and biennials used in cottage gardens are richly scented, including such plants as wallflowers, candytuft and sweet William. Vegetables and herbs are very much part of cottage garden planting and at this time of year you can expect to see paths edged with pink-flowered chives, pot marigolds, variegated mints, bright gold marjoram and the dusky new growth of bronze and green fennel.

There are many plants to choose from for the woodland garden. On moist, acid soil around yellow, orange and flame-colored deciduous azaleas, grow the white-flowered wake robin (*Trillium grandiflorum*) and shade-loving bulbs, such as blue-flowered quamash (*Camassia*) and bluebells, alongside blue-leaved hostas and the yellow-mottled piggyback plant (*Tolmiea*). Orange and yellow Welsh poppies (*Meconopsis*) will also happily colonize these conditions.

Above left: In a moist shady border, blue *Iris sibirica* grows alongside cerise primulas, acid-green alchemilla and blue geraniums in a riot of color in early summer.

Right: An early summer planting of Jacob's ladder (*Polemonium*), *Geranium clarkei* 'Kashmir White', silver artemisia and pink cow parsley. The drumstick allium, *A. hollandicum*, forms a link between the spring and summer garden.

LATE SPRING PERENNIALS FOR MOIST GROUND

Carex elata 'Aurea'

Euphorbia griffithii 'Fireglow'

Hosta

Houttuynia cordata 'Chameleon'

Iris chrysographes

Iris ensata

Iris sibirica

Lysimachia nummularia 'Aurea'

Persicaria bistorta 'Superba'

Rheum palmatum 'Atrosanguineum'

Zantedeschia aethiopica 'Crowborough'

LATE SPRING PERENNIALS FOR SHADE

Aconitum 'Ivorine'

Corydalis flexuosa

Dicentra

Geranium phaeum

Hesperis matronalis

Iris, Pacific Coast and Californian hybrids

Lamium maculatum

Meconopsis cambrica

Polygonatum x *hybridum*

Saxifraga x *urbium*

Smilacina racemosa

Tolmeia menziesii 'Taff's Gold'

Trillium

Veratrum nigrum

Viola cornuta

Viola hybrids

By the end of June, you know just by looking at the garden that spring has made the long-awaited transition into summer. Flowering trees such as lilac, cherry, crab apple and laburnum have come to the end of their display along with the rhododendrons and azaleas, weigela and wisteria. The last tulip has faded and the foliage of spring bulbs is dying down, camouflaged by strategically-planted perennials.

The traditional herbaceous border reaches it's peak in early summer with bearded irises, geraniums, bleeding heart, oriental poppies, peonies and giant white clouds of *Crambe cordifolia*.

Gradually these blooms give way to other familiar plants such as *Anthemis*, spires of soft blue bellflowers, sea hollies, achilleas and daylilies. Some early perennials continue to make an important contribution by way of their handsome leaves, long after the blooms have faded. Taller iris cultivars and peonies, with their handsome divided foliage, are valuable for this reason. Drumstick alliums also have an enduring quality as the flowers turn into everlasting seedheads that provide sculptural interest for months to come.

In most climates, annuals are also flowering well by July. In regions experiencing late spring frosts and an early fall, it's important to choose annuals that mature rapidly so that you can enjoy the longest possible display of flowers. Some annuals look very like herbaceous perennials and blend in easily in the mixed border.

Midsummer sees the arrival of lupines and vivid blue delphinium cultivars. Grown well they make an eye-catching spectacle in the June and July border, but the over-bred delphiniums in particular need careful staking and cosseting to thrive and lupine plants rapidly degenerate after flowering and take up a lot of space with their uninspiring foliage. There are so many other plants to choose from, with a longer season of interest that it is hard to justify their inclusion in today's mixed borders.

In midsummer, the scent of roses mingles with that of white-flowered mock oranges (*Philadelphus*) and later on with the butterfly bush (*Buddleja davidii*). There are fragrant climbers too, such as honeysuckles and jasmine (*Jasminum officinale*). Unfortunately just as the flowers grow, so do the weeds and it can be a hard struggle to keep things under control. On free-draining sandy soils in particular, the garden may suffer through lack of water unless you have taken steps to prevent it. Growth slows and without planning, flowers become less numerous just when you're wanting to spend more time outdoors enjoying the warmer weather. The days are relatively hot and dry and plants which tolerate these conditions are welcomed by today's drought-conscious gardeners. Happily some plants just keep on going all summer long, whatever the weather.

the main event

Summer is the season we spend most time outdoors and, fortunately, this is also the time when most perennials bloom. It is easy to create a colorful display at this time of year and there's also a wealth of foliage to enhance blooms and provide texture.

Far left: A Provence-style garden in early summer featuring deep mauve irises, purple alliums and French lavender which enliven a cobbled terrace.

Above: Blue and white bellflowers (*Campanula*) in an informal display.

PLANTS FOR MIDSUMMER

There are many perennials that begin flowering from early to midsummer, which make perfect partners for roses because of their complementary coloring, texture and overall habit. These are plants with a very different flower shape or arrangement of blooms, such as bell-shaped flowers set in slender spires or many small blooms in large branching heads. Leaves that are feathery, elegantly cut, narrow, strap-shaped or sword-like also provide good contrast. Lavender and lilac-blue, mauve, white and green-flowered perennials as well as ones with silver, purple or bronze foliage go very well with most roses. Try early-flowering roses with a frothy underplanting of lime-green lady's mantle, and forms of horned violet (*Viola cornuta*) or catmint (*Nepeta* x *faassenii*), with the enchanting silver carpeting lamb's ears (*Stachys byzantina*).

Plants with tall upright stems such as foxgloves, hollyhocks, mulleins (*Verbascum*), lilies, certain bellflowers, daylilies and feathery bronze fennel make pleasing partnerships with larger-growing roses. One of the best for planting in groups among repeat-flowering shrub roses is *Campanula lactiflora*, whose violet-blue cultivar, 'Prichard's Variety', has stems reaching 4–5 feet, blooming from early summer to late fall. The large branching heads are made up of many starry bell flowers and, being slightly top heavy, may need staking in windy areas.

On a smaller scale and much more delicate in appearance is the peach-leaved bellflower, *C. persicifolia*. It sends up wiry stems with relatively large lilac-blue bellflowers arranged in loose spikes. Growing to only 3 feet tall it is useful for foreground planting, helping to cover bare stem bases. There is a beautiful white form and both are easily raised from seed. These plants have a cottage-garden feel, but there are many campanulas now becoming more widely available that would sit happily with almost any style. They include the cool and elegant, white-flowered *Campanula alliariifolia*, and the very handsome speckled *C. takesimana*.

Above: Catmint makes a wonderful foil for yellow and pink bush roses.

Top: Blue chairs contrast with the surrounding planting of yellow *Achillea filipendulina* 'Gold Plate', *Hemerocallis* 'Stafford' and *Rudbeckia fulgida*.

Many of the blue or violet-flowered hardy geraniums (cranesbills) bloom in May and June, after which time the handsome foliage provides continuing interest. A large cranesbill that flowers somewhat later in midsummer is the glowing magenta *Geranium psilostemon*. Its large dish-shaped blooms have a prominent black eye and the elegantly-cut leaves have good fall tinting. If you want a similar effect at the front of the border, choose the spreading 'Anne Folkard', which only grows to 12 inches. In spring the leaves are bright acid green. Many other geraniums flower during the summer months, such as the pink *Geranium* x *oxonianum*, often used as border edging and for ground cover, and the carpeting *Geranium* x *riversleaianum* 'Russell Prichard'.

Daylilies are easy to grow and most, with the exception of the evergreen kinds, are hardy and reliable. Some of the taller, large-flowered ones are almost as exotic looking as lilies and several are deliciously scented. Cultivars with a simple sculpted flower form in a clear bright color can look quite contemporary, blooming as they do over substantial clumps of strap-shaped leaves. Equally, those in softer shades with ruffled or rounded petals work well in a period scheme.

MIDSUMMER FLOWERS

Perennials for a well-drained soil
Achillea

Anthemis tinctoria

Campanula

Cerinthe major 'Purpurascens'

Coreopsis verticillata 'Moonbeam'

Crambe maritima

Erigeron

Geranium nodosum

Geranium psilostemon

x *Heucherella alba* 'Bridget Bloom'

Knautia macedonica

Leucanthemum x *superbum*

Malva moschata 'Alba'

Salvia x *superba*

Stachys macrantha

Viola cornuta

Annuals, Biennials and Tender Perennials
Alcea rosea

Antirrhinum

Argyranthemum

Atriplex hortensis rubra

Bidens ferulifolia

Brachycombe iberidifolia

Calendula officinalis

Cosmos

Digitalis purpurea

Eschscholzia californica

Fuchsia

Impatiens

Lavatera trimestris

Mimulus hybridus

Nicotiana

Nigella damascena

Osteospermum

Papaver

Rudbeckia

Salvia coccinea 'Lady in Red'

Salvia farinacea

Verbena

71

DROUGHT-RESISTANT PERENNIALS

Midsummer Interest

Alchemilla mollis

Armeria

Ballota

Centranthus ruber

Erigeron karvinskianus

Eryngium

Geranium cinereum 'Ballerina'

Lychnis coronaria

Oenothera speciosa

Phlomis russeliana

Sisyrinchium striatum

Thymus

Verbascum

Late Summer Interest

Acaena saccaticupula 'Blue Haze'

Acanthus spinosus

Artemisia

Convolvulus sabatius

Erigeron karvinskianus

Festuca

Foeniculum vulgare 'Purpureum'

Helictotrichon sempervirens

Liatris spicata

Nepeta

Oenothera fruticosa

Oenothera macrocarpa

Oenothera speciosa 'Rosea'

Ophiopogon planiscapus 'Nigrescens'

Origanum

Osteospermum jucundum

Penstemon

Perovskia 'Blue Spire'

Rhodanthemum hosmariense

Romneya coulteri

Salvia officinalis

Scabiosa 'Butterfly Blue' and 'Pink Mist'

Sedum

Stachys byzantina

Stipa

DROUGHT-TOLERANT PLANTS FOR SUMMER

In a hot, dry border in midsummer, one of the most strikingly-architectural plants is the sea holly or eryngo (*Eryngium*). With their sculpted blooms and metallic coloring, eryngos have a very modern feel, and this perhaps explains their popularity in recent years. Some form large heads of very small ball-shaped blooms with thorny collars, while others have large thimble-shaped heads. One of the best of this type is *Eryngium alpinum* with 2-inch tall thimbles surmounted by a lacy ruff of bracts all in a remarkable blue-tinged purple that extends down the flower stems. Even more richly colored is the shorter-growing *Eryngium* x *zabelii* 'Violetta' which as its name suggests is a glowing violet. For deep blue flowers and rather beautiful, silver-marbled leaves try one of the many decorative forms of *Eryngium bourgatii* such as 'Oxford Blue'.

Fortunately there's a wealth of other drought-tolerant plants to use all round the garden in summer. To soften the edges of gravel paths or to colonize the cracks between paving try aromatic thymes, the daisy-flowered *Erigeron karvinskianus*, sea pinks (*Armeria*) and low-growing evening primroses (*Oenothera*). Taller plants, including the deep cerise-flowered dusty miller (*Lychnis*), red valerian (*Centranthus*), verbascums and airy-flowered ornamental grasses, can also be used right at the front to break up the monotony of a border that is too rigidly graded by height. For an impressive specimen further back in the border try bear's breeches (*Acanthus spinosus*), which makes a mound of deep glossy green, deeply-cut leaves, a perfect foil for the stately flower spikes. Equally eye-catching is the cardoon; its enormous, jaggedly-cut silver leaves are impressive well before the thistle-like heads appear.

High summer is the time when you get most enjoyment out of aromatic plants and herbs because heat helps to release their volatile oils into the atmosphere. Traditionally, enclosed herb gardens were centered around a pool with a simple fountain, the humidity helping to capture the aromas. You could create a Mediterranean garden planted with aromatic and drought-tolerant shrubs, herbs, grasses and alpines, with a seating area set beneath a jasmine-covered pergola. Add the sound of gently trickling water and you will have created a perfect summer garden oasis. Plant with fragrant shrubs, such as lavender, rosemary, cotton lavender (*Santolina*), sun rose (*Cistus*) and Spanish broom (*Spartium junceum*). Add to this structure bronze fennel, thymes for flowering and foliage interest, ornamental marjorams, ornamental sages, catmints, silvery artemisias and the late-blooming Russian sage (*Perovskia*).

Compact, long-flowering or foliage perennials with reasonable drought tolerance are also good for pots on the terrace or deck. The creeping diascias are ideal and look lovely grown with the trailing stems of the blue-flowered *Convolvulus sabatius*. In a large pot you could center this arrangement with the silvery sword-shaped leaves of *Astelia chathamica*. For a yellow and blue scheme try golden thyme as a foil for *Scabiosa* 'Butterfly Blue'. Blue African lilies (*Agapanthus*) also look striking when grown in pots and are best planted singly for the most dramatic effect. Other perennials to plant as specimens in tubs and other containers include daisy-flowered *Osteospermum jucundum*, which thrives in a very sunny site, *Rhodanthemum hosmariense* and blue or gray-leaved grasses.

Left: Sun-loving, drought-tolerant plants, including herbs and silver-leaved plants, are combined in these pretty pastel-shaded borders.

Above left: Penstemons, such as 'Sour Grapes', are colorful plants for dry areas, and flower reliably through summer.

Above: This striking blue, yellow and silver scheme uses blue geraniums, silver *Artemisia latiloba* 'Silver Queen' and yellow evening primrose, all of which tolerate dry conditions in summer.

SUMMER SHADE

Most shade plants bloom in spring and early summer but there are perennials that will lighten the gloom in high summer. Combined with shrubs, these can help to create a cool haven from the midday sun. It's worth improving the moisture-holding capacity of the soil since most shade-loving plants grow more luxuriantly on moisture-retentive ground. Many hydrangeas flower over a long period beginning in July and make a wonderful backdrop for shade-loving perennials. Examples are the cream *Hydrangea arborescens* 'Annabelle' or the hortensia, *H. macrophylla* 'Madame Emile Mouillère', which has white blooms gradually becoming pink tinged. For foliage try the yellow-leaved dogwood, *Cornus alba* 'Aurea', the yellow-variegated *Weigela florida* 'Aureovariegata' or the white-variegated elder, *Sambucus nigra* 'Marginata'. Then all you need to do is to introduce layers of foliage and flower in the form of perennials.

Goat's beard (*Aruncus*) makes a large, leafy specimen up to 7 feet high with creamy plumes in midsummer. Then there are hostas such as 'Royal Standard' with white flowers and the pale lilac 'Honeybells', both of which bloom in late summer. The master-worts (*Astrantia*) would also make worthy additions to the scene, especially the large-flowered 'Shaggy' with its distinctive cream and green blooms. To cover a large area at the foot of shrubs, try the vigorous magenta-pink flowered *Geranium* x *oxonianum* 'Claridge Druce', which flowers for many weeks and has ever-green leaves, or the shorter 'Wargrave

Left: *Hosta fortunei albopicta* with purple heuchera 'Palace Purple'.

Below: *Geranium* x *oxonianum* 'Wargrave Pink'.

Bottom: *Persicaria amplexicaulis* 'Firetail'.

Pink' with salmon-pink blooms well into the fall. And at ground level try a carpet of silver-leaved lamium. The white-flowered form of horned violet and the pink-flowered x *Heucherella alba* 'Bridget Bloom' also make good foreground plants.

In a lightly-shaded bog garden, broad-leaved perennials like rodgersia, hostas, *Inula magnifica* and the umbrella plant, *Darmera peltata*, would make a lush backdrop for the fluffy plumes of fern-leaved astilbes. Astilbes vary in their flowering time, so if you choose carefully you can enjoy them for most of the summer. Red and purple-flowered cultivars make a striking combination with the mahogany leaves and orange-blooms of *Ligularia dentata* 'Desdemona'. In

a border with moist, rather than waterlogged soil, many of the above plants would survive perfectly well, they just wouldn't grow so large.

Some summer-flowering perennials prefer growing in moisture-retentive soil and in such conditions are happy in full sun. For a richly-colored and architectural scheme try purple monarda, violet-purple wand flower (*Dierama pulcherrimum*), and the crimson-red knotweed, *Persicaria amplexicaulis* 'Firetail', mixed with the solid shapes of green-flowered *Angelica archangelica*, tall yellow daylily cultivars (*Hemerocallis*), the handsome yellow-striped bamboo, *Pleioblastus auricomus*, and the stately golden-variegated zebra grass, *Miscanthus sinensis* 'Zebrinus'.

PLANTS FOR MOIST GROUND

Alchemilla mollis
Angelica archangelica
Aruncus
Astrantia
Dierama pulcherrimum
Hemerocallis
Hosta
Inula
Lamium
Ligularia dentata
Miscanthus sinensis
Persicaria amplexicaulis
Pleioblastus
Rheum palmatum
Rodgersia

PLANTS FOR THE BOG GARDEN

Astilbe
Astilboides tabularis
Darmera peltata
Hosta
Houttuynia cordata 'Chameleon'
Iris ensata
Ligularia
Mentha
Rodgersia

LATE SUMMER PERENNIALS

Plants for a well-drained soil

Agapanthus

Artemisia lactiflora

Astelia chathamica

Aster × frikartii 'Mönch'

Cynara cardunculus

Diascia

Echinacea purpurea

Echinops

Euphorbia

Gaura lindheimeri

Geranium × oxonianum

Geranium × riversleaianum

Geranium wallichianum

Heuchera

Kniphofia

Libertia peregrinans

Macleaya

Platycodon grandiflorus

Salvia verticillata 'Purple Rain'

Verbena bonariensis

Veronicastrum virginicum album

Plants for moist soil

Aconitum

Carex elata 'Aurea'

Carex oshimensis 'Evergold'

Cimicifuga

Crocosmia

Deschampsia

Hakonechloa macra 'Aureola'

Hemerocallis

Holcus mollis 'Albovariegatus'

Inula magnifica

Miscanthus sinensis

Molinia caerulea arundinacea 'Variegata'

Monarda

Persicaria amplexicaulis 'Firetail'

Pleioblastus auricomus

Rudbeckia

Schizostylis coccinea

Veratrum

LATE SUMMER

In a sunny, well-drained border that doesn't dry out in summer, several groups of perennials begin a welcome display that begins around August. Their appearance serves to rejuvenate the late summer border. The first of these is crocosmia, with its arching red, orange or yellow flower sprays above grassy clumps creating a vivid splash of color. The brilliant flame-red 'Lucifer' is the most dramatic and one of the tallest with handsome sword-like leaves. It works well in large stands between other perennials that help to support it. Try it in front of the tall blue-flowered globe thistle, *Echinops bannaticus* 'Taplow Blue', or the orange-tinted plume poppy, *Macleaya microcarpa* 'Kelway's Coral Plume'. Shorter-growing crocosmias go well at the front of a mixed border and this is also the best position for the blue African lily, *Agapanthus*, whose long smooth stems curve out toward the light carrying large rounded heads of tubular flowers. The leaves are grassy in dwarf cultivars, fleshy arching and strap shaped in taller kinds. Select hardier cultivars from specialist nurseries, particularly if you live in colder regions.

Red hot pokers flower from June to October depending on the type, but a larger proportion bloom in late summer through to fall. There are forms with green, cream, yellow, orange or red flowers and others with creamy pokers tipped brown or coral pink. Many of the cultivars make substantial plants between 3 and 4 feet tall, with strongly-upright stems and coarse foliage. But the dainty 'Little Maid' has slender cream pokers over grassy hummocks and is a delight at the front of the late summer border.

One of the most important of all the late summer perennial flowers is the beard tongue or penstemon. It needs a warm sunny site, sheltered from cold spring gales, and fertile

Left: Kniphofia 'Little Maid', Penstemon 'Alice Hindley', and Hemerocallis 'Joan Senior' make a colorful display in a late summer border.

Above left: Grasses like Miscanthus sinensis 'Morning Light' put on a handsome show of foliage right though summer until the fall.

Above: Hemerocallis 'Mrs David Hall' with a backdrop of kniphofia.

free-draining soil without so much as a hint of waterlogging in winter. These bushy, evergreen perennials come in white and a myriad of pink, red and purple shades. They are long flowered and you can make them repeat if you steel yourself and remove the stems before the spikes have completely finished flowering. You can normally see clearly where the secondary spikes are growing out at the base. Different penstemon cultivars can be massed in the border to breathtaking effect but the tall spires combine with any number of flower shapes from the stiff, daisy-like

cone flowers (*Echinacea purpurea*) to flat-headed achilleas. They also work well with insubstantial blooms such as those of catmints and calamints, diascias, cranesbills and the airy *Gaura lindheimeri*.

The light in late summer is quite hard. It tends to wash out soft pastels, at the same time enlivening hot scarlet, magenta, cerise, plum, orange, salmon-pink and yellow. Smoky-purple and bronze-tinted foliage works well with these flower shades and schemes that include saturated colors blend happily with those of fall, making an easy transition from one season to the next.

COLD-CLIMATE MULCHES

Summertime mulches keep weeds down and conserve moisture. In cold climates, the soil takes longer to warm up in spring, so do not mulch too early or it will delay the warming process — wait until mid-June. One of the easiest mulches is grass mowings, but only use them if you don't use herbicides. Fresh clippings may have little pieces of root attached, which could take root, so spread the clippings out on a hard surface to dry out. When brown, mulch to a depth of 2 inches.

Fall is a magical season. Colors glow in the gentle golden light, silvers sparkle, and greens appear richer. The leaves of many shrubs and trees begin to turn, with golden-yellow, orange, red and deep maroon-purple tones. At the same time, the romantic papery blooms of hydrangeas develop shading like old tapestry. Herbaceous perennials do not immediately spring to mind when thinking about fall color, but many undergo a similar kind of alchemy as they begin to die down or, in the case of evergreens, as they experience cooler temperatures.

Although by September the nights are noticeably colder and there's a distinct chill in the morning air, the days are often still warm and pleasant. Most half-hardy annuals, and particularly the tender perennials including dahlias and fuchsias, are still flowering in earnest and will do so until the first major frosts (in mild maritime climates that may not be until late November or December). Some annuals such as the pastel-shaded Chinese asters (*Callistephus*) are at their best in late summer and early fall. Within this group of late performers, the cone flowers (*Rudbeckia*) reign supreme. In shades of orange, rusty-brown and yellow, they echo the fall leaf colors. The orange-flowered 'Marmalade' fits in well with

late arrivals

Fall is an atmospheric season when the garden is rich in color and texture. While there are blooms around, the foliage of many perennials becomes colorful, and ornamental seedheads add an extra dimension, particularly when highlighted by frost.

perennials in the border and the newer dwarfs like 'Becky', 'Toto' and 'Sonora' are perfect for edging.

Of course some annuals will have gone over by fall, and should be cleared away if they begin to look unsightly. In general though, this is a time of year when you need to develop a relaxed attitude to the garden and

not be over-tidy. Cut plants back too soon, and you could miss out on the subtle changes in leaf color or the beauty of the developing seedheads. In mild gardens without much snow, it's important to keep as much structure in the garden as you can to add interest through the winter months. The sight of frosted stems and flower heads is breathtaking. Foliage left to die down over the crowns of perennials acts as natural insulation and, in any case, pulls away more easily in spring.

Along with bush roses, a considerable number of summer-flowering perennials continues to bloom, encouraged by regular deadheading. At the same time, fall-flowering bulbs and late perennials bring a fresh wave of color. You can combine their blooms with flowering or berrying shrubs to wonderful effect and use purple and blue flowers to complement fall foliage colors. In the woodland garden, bulbs in large drifts look magical when pushing up through the carpet of leaves. Shade-tolerant herbaceous plants can be used in a similar way to give the illusion of wild colonies.

As the leaves fall, the bark color and texture of certain shrubs and trees becomes more prominent and can be further highlighted with an underplanting or foreground of bulbs

Far left: Many cranesbills develop rich tints in the fall. Those of *Geranium wlassovianum* are as colorful as any flower.

Above: The seedheads of *Allium christophii* look like globes of tiny stars.

Above right: Ornamental grasses pictured after a fall frost include a tall *Miscanthus* with nodding tassels, and *Pennisetum alpecuroides* with arching bottle brush flowers.

Right: Evergreen perennials, such as this silver-speckled lungwort (*Pulmonaria saccharata*) are most valuable in the fall, carpeting bare ground and providing a foil for late blooms.

and perennials. If in fall you add to the display with some spring-flowering bulbs and some evergreen, spring-flowering perennials, you can create a two season display with just a quiet summer period in between.

A Japanese or eastern-style garden can look beautiful in the fall with the colored leaves of trees and shrubs reflected in a still pond. Lush bog garden specimens, such as the umbrella plant (*Darmera*), rodgersias, rheum and moisture-loving ferns, begin to display rich tints and hostas of all kinds slowly turn butter yellow, their leaves becoming almost translucent as they die down.

In shaded moss gardens, beneath a light tree canopy with Japanese maples and low, hummock-forming evergreen azaleas, create a splash of color with a clump of *Iris foetidissima*, the large pods of which split open in the fall to reveal bright orange berries. Carpets of barrenwort (*Epimedium*) would also work well here, the heart-shaped leaves of many kinds coloring in the fall and lasting all through winter. Toad lilies (*Tricyrtis*) also have an appropriately oriental look and would form a subtle picture, seen against a backdrop of lacecap hydrangeas or combined with the foliage of winter and spring-flowering hellebores and evergreen ferns. As a low foreground you could plant a carpet of hardy cyclamen (*Cyclamen hederifolium*).

Evergreen perennials with strong architectural form are particularly effective grouped informally in areas mulched with gravel or pebbles. Try bold clumps of plants like bergenia, ornamental sedges including yellow-striped *Carex oshimensis* 'Evergold',

black-leaved *Ophiopogon* and red-stemmed *Helleborus foetidus* 'Wester Flisk'. All of these plants will take sun or shade. From the very large group of ornamental grasses, select those with a Far Eastern feel such as the lower-growing, tassel-headed forms of Japanese silver grass.

The graceful flowers of many ornamental grasses like deschampsia, molinia, stipa and miscanthus, turn to shades of parchment and gold in the fall. Planted singly or in small

groups, they make a pleasing contrast with fall blooms of other perennials in the sunny border, particularly ones that have a bold form or which give the impression of solidity. Try them with early fall-flowering red hot pokers like *Kniphofia triangularis* or *K. uvaria*, taller sedums such as 'Herbstfreude' ('Autumn Joy'), with the 'everlasting' spikes of bear's breeches or with the stiff golden daisy-like flowers of *Rudbeckia fulgida sullivantii* 'Goldsturm'. Golden oats (*Stipa*

gigantea) makes a striking specimen with silver-leaved plants, cushions of aromatic calamint and thyme and plants with sword-shaped foliage such as phormiums in a Mediterranean-style gravel garden. And the fine blue foliage of fescues and blue oat grass (*Helictotrichon sempervirens*) looks marvelous against a backdrop of amber, yellow, scarlet or orange fall leaves and berries

Another way to grow grasses is to devote an area of the garden to them with gravel pathways or a wooden board walk and perhaps an informal pool or cobble stream running through to give the impression of moisture. Such an area would need

very careful planning to be effective because grasses have a similar texture to one another. Plant in bold blocks or swathes to really show off the form of the plants and maximize the show of flowers. Make sure adjacent groups vary in height, color, flower and habit.

Apart from grasses, many other perennials have long-lasting seedheads and stems. Some are bold enough to be effective as single plants, such as the sculpted silver thimbles of sea holly (*Eryngium giganteum*) or the upright stems and whorled flower bracts of *Phlomis russeliana*. Others need to be seen as a bold swathe of seedheads, such as astilbe cultivars in a waterside or bog planting.

PERENNIALS WITH FALL-TINTED FOLIAGE

Bergenia
Ceratostigma willmottianum
Darmera peltata
Epimedium
Euphorbia dulcis 'Chameleon'
Euphorbia griffithii 'Fireglow'
Geranium macrorrhizum
Geranium x *magnificum*
Geranium wlassovianum
Hosta
Libertia peregrinans
Osmunda regalis
Paeonia
Rodgersia
Sedum aizoon

PERENNIALS WITH SEEDHEADS OR SKELETAL FORM

Acaena saccaticupula 'Blue Haze'
Acanthus spinosus
Agapanthus
Allium
Astilbe
Ballota
Baptisia australis
Deschampsia caespitosa
Eryngium
Iris foetidissima
Iris sibirica
Matteuccia struthiopteris
Miscanthus sinensis
Osmunda regalis
Pennisetum orientale
Phlomis russeliana
Rudbeckia
Sedum
Stipa calamagrostis
Stipa gigantea

PERENNIALS THAT COME INTO BLOOM IN THE FALL

Aconitum

Anemone hupehensis

Anemone x hybrida

Aster ericoides

Aster lateriflorus 'Horizontalis'

Aster 'Ringdove'

Aster turbinellus

Calamintha nepeta

Ceratostigma willmottianum

Kniphofia

Liriope muscari

Pennisetum alopecuroides

Schizostylis coccinea

Sedum 'Bertram Anderson'

Sedum 'Herbstfreude' ('Autumn Joy')

Sedum 'Ruby Glow'

Sedum spectabile

Sedum 'Vera Jameson'

Tricyrtis

LONG-FLOWERED PERENNIALS THAT BLOOM INTO FALL

Aster x frikartii 'Mönch'

Campanula lactiflora

Diascia

Echinacea purpurea

Gaura lindheimeri

Geranium

Oenothera macrocarpa

Oenothera speciosa 'Rosea'

Penstemon

Persicaria amplexicaulis 'Firetail'

Platycodon grandiflorus

Rhodanthemum hosmariense

Romneya coulteri

Rudbeckia

Scabiosa 'Butterfly Blue'

Verbena bonariensis

LATE BLOOMS

Late-flowering perennials are always very welcome, adding a note of freshness to the often rather jaded late summer garden. Some, like the Japanese anemones, straddle both seasons beginning to bloom in August and continuing into September. These elegant perennials make spreading clumps of grape vine-shaped leaves above which slender stems bear spherical buds and open dish-shaped blooms. They mainly come in shades of light pastel pink and mauve, though some, such as 'Bressingham Glow' and 'Margarete' are a deep, rich pink. Japanese anemones are effective colonizers, and can be allowed to weave their way between plants in an established shrub border. Try them with berrying shrubs like orange-fruited firethorns and *Rosa* 'Geranium' which has clusters of large, flask-shaped red hips.

Since purple is the complementary color for orange on the color wheel (see page 46), you can see that purple or blue-flowered herbaceous perennials

and bulbs would work well with all the fall leaf and berry colors around. Monkshoods (*Aconitum*), asters, lily turf, crocuses and colchicums, calamints, *Verbena bonariensis* and certain late-flowering penstemon cultivars all produce blooms in shades of purple and burgundy. And to that list you can also add purple foliage perennials including various sedums and *Viola labradorica*. For vibrant blues there are perennials like the fall-flowering gentian, *Gentiana sino-ornata*, Chinese plumbago, balloon flower (*Platy-*

codon), and late-flowering shrubs including cultivars of *Caryopteris* x *clandonensis*, *Hibiscus syriacus* 'Oiseau Bleu' ('Blue Bird') and, on acid soil, many mop-head and lacecap hydrangea cultivars. The soft blue and white-flowered *Geranium wallichianum* 'Buxton's Variety' would make a wonderful carpet in front of *Fothergilla major* or beneath the spreading branches of a witch hazel.

Silver foliage provides sparkle in the low fall sunshine. It works well with blue and purple flowers and the classic fall colors of leaves and berries and also complements rich red, burnt orange and crimson blooms. As well as low, sun-loving evergreen shrubs such as cotton lavender (*Santolina chamaecyparissus*) and the aromatic curry plant (*Helichrysum italicum*), there are felted lamb's ears (*Stachys*), the dainty filigree-cut artemisias and *Rhodanthemum hosmariense*.

It's easy to create yellow and red schemes in the fall using flowering and berrying shrubs and herbaceous perennials. Try combining the translucent berries of the guelder rose (*Viburnum opulus* 'Xanthocarpum') with the rich red spires of *Persicaria amplexicaulis* 'Firetail' and ground cover in the form of *Geranium maccrorhizum* or *G. wlassovianum*, whose semi-evergreen leaves develop bright fall tints. The yellow and green striped low-growing bamboo *Pleioblastus auricomus* also is looking good at this time of year and would work well in such a setting. The scheme could continue through late fall with one of the cultivars of the yellow-flowered *Mahonia* x *media* and a berried firethorn or cotoneaster.

For a yellow and blue scheme, you could combine *Hypericum* 'Hidcote', with the arching foliage of variegated Pampas grass (*Cortaderia selloana* 'Aureolineata') and low carpets of the golden yellow-variegated *Euonymus fortunei* with blocks of *Aster* x *frikartii* 'Mönch', the delicate Aster *ericoides* 'Blue Star' and blue balloon flower (*Platycodon*) planted in between.

Left: Speckled toad lilies (*Tricyrtis formosana*) have small but intricate blooms that are worth close examination. They thrive in woodland soil and combine well with berrying shrubs.

Below far left: The trouble-free Aster x *frikartii* 'Mönch' blooms through summer and well into fall, with a profusion of lavender-blue flowers.

Below center: The lily turf, *Liriope muscari*, is a useful, late-flowering perennial often used for edging paths.

Below: Japanese anemones are a feature in this border in late summer and early fall. White is effective when light levels drop toward the end of the year.

The great thing about the majority of plants mentioned in this book is that they do not require a great deal of maintenance. And if you choose the right plant for a particular situation, you should avoid many of the problems that gardeners are so often faced with. Plants that are growing strongly with the correct levels of light, moisture and nutrition will often manage to fight off pest and disease attacks unaided. It's not an exact science and some plants simply won't thrive in your garden. You may never find out why. Sometimes moving a plant to a spot just a few feet away does the trick and it's often only when you dig up an ailing specimen that you discover that the true reason for it's poor performance is damage to the roots. The health of the parts of the plant below the soil surface is frequently overlooked.

Many plants can be left in peace once planted. But some burn themselves out after only a few years of furious flowering, literally draining the soil of necessary nutrients or producing too many unproductive old, woody stems and filling the soil with matted roots. These plants respond very well to being lifted and divided. You can spot when this rejuvenation is needed because the center of the plant begins to look bare and doesn't produce as

essential care

Given the right spot, many perennials are easy to care for and maintenance is generally routine. Happily, there are plenty of ways to cut down on chores such as watering and weeding, leaving you with more time to simply enjoy the garden.

much new growth as the perimeter of the clump. Discard the central portion and split the remaining rootstock into chunks for replanting. Each chunk must have a good section of healthy root and some top growth. This is also a good way of propagating the majority of herbaceous perennials. Do any division in fall when the soil is still

quite warm and moist, providing ideal conditions for root growth, or in spring, which is a better time for cold regions. If you are planning to replant in the same spot, apply a slow-release fertilizer with trace elements, or plenty of well-rotted manure to replace some of the leached nutrients. Avoid growing members of the same family in the same spot year after year as pests and diseases are liable to build up and certain key nutrients will get used up, leaving the soil poor.

To keep the garden looking tidy and to encourage repeat bloom, remove spent blossoms – a process called deadheading – regularly. This is one of the best ways to promote continued flowering. It also helps to keep displays looking fresh and lessens the risk of fungal disease. Several plants benefit from being cut back hard midway through the season. For soft-stemmed plants you can usually do this with a normal nylon-line "weed whacker" or with garden shears. Provided you water thoroughly afterward and apply a liquid feed to boost regrowth, the plants should produce a handsome, long-lasting crop of fresh new leaves and even flowers. Cut back the plants as soon as the foliage begins to look a little jaded and flowering performance is beginning to fall off.

Far left: A display such as this requires proper planning and soil preparation. Once established, plants need annual maintenance, but regular "preening" is worthwhile, if you have sufficient time.

1. To divide a clump of perennials, lift the plant carefully, levering it out with a garden fork.

2. Shake off the soil and separate the crowns, discarding the oldest. Choose healthy portions with good roots attached.

3. Replenish the soil with well-rotted manure or a general-purpose fertilizer.

4. Spread out the roots in the new planting hole and back-fill with good soil.

5. Firm in gently with your foot, then water copiously.

new growth coming from the base while existing stems usually look rather jaded. Cut out these old stems just above the regrowth. At the same time cut back the stems of dwarf creeping bamboos like *Pleioblastus auricomus* and the sedge, *Carex buchananii*, to ground level. The resultant regrowth will be much stronger and more brightly colored.

MAINTAINING FERTILITY

Because of the way that herbaceous perennials die back to ground level each year, you end up removing large amounts of plant matter from the beds as part of routine maintenance. This also occurs when clearing weeds and annual flowers. Nutrients and trace elements are locked up in this detritus and, unless they are replaced, the soil gradually becomes impoverished. On fertile clay soils this may not be a problem for some years, but on light sandy soils, especially in areas of high rainfall, nutrients tend to be in rather short supply.

In order to maintain fertility, you need to either apply an annual dressing of a balanced slow-release fertilizer with trace elements as growth commences in spring or to mulch with garden compost, spent mushroom or seaweed compost or well-rotted animal manure in late winter or early spring.

Mulching also improves soil structure and helps to conserve moisture. But you do need to be a little careful with animal manure. If not sufficiently well rotted, it can scorch foliage, and straw that is insufficiently broken down actually extracts nutrients while it is decomposing. Straw also may contain herbicide residues that

Some plants produce several main flowering spikes with embryonic branches lower down – these can often be detected as tufts of small new leaves. If the central spike is cut back to just above these branches as soon as it begins to fade, this encourages them to grow, producing a lesser but still

important flowering display. Plants include *Aconitum* (monkshood), *Campanula* (bellflower), penstemon, verbascum, foxglove and salvia.

In mild regions, a few perennials remain evergreen and, in the case of penstemons, become quite bushy and woody. In spring you'll notice a lot of

Above: Some perennials will produce smaller, lateral flower spikes if you remove the main spike as the flowers fade.

Left: Mulleins (*Verbascum*) often respond to this treament (above).

Right: Other perennials also respond to deadheading. Remove spent blooms as they fade.

1. To maintain fertility in new or existing beds, apply a balanced slow-release fertilizer, following manufacturer's instructions.

2. Alternatively, mulch with well-rotted garden compost or animal manure in spring.

can stunt the growth of perennials. Manure that has been set aside for three years is ideal as a soil conditioner, but if it has been stored uncovered, it may have had some of the valuable nutrients washed out by rain.

In addition to annual treatments, you can use liquid feeds as a boost for growth midseason, especially on impoverished soils. Granular fertilizers need to be watered in if there is insufficient rainfall so liquid feeds are ideal during the summer months. Look for a product that contains a higher proportion of potassium that increases flower production rather than nitrogen which stimulates leafy growth in plants. Do not feed after the end of August as the new shoots that grow in response will not have time to harden sufficiently before the onset of winter. And remember, whenever you feed ornamental plants you will also be feeding the weeds, so apply sparingly.

PLANTS TO CUT BACK MIDSEASON

Alchemilla mollis

Centaurea montana

Centranthus ruber

Erigeron karvinskianus

Geranium x oxonianum

Lamium maculatum

Mentha

Nepeta x faassenii

Pulmonaria

Rhodanthemum hosmariense

Viola cornuta

Above: When alchemilla flowers begin to look tired, shear over the whole plant to encourage fresh new leaves and new flowers to form.

MOISTURE CONSERVATION

Shortage of water during the growing season can have an even more devastating effect on growth than shortage of fertilizer. If your soil is light and free draining, and you live in a low rainfall area, especially if there are local restrictions on irrigation, you need to develop a strategy for coping. Choose drought-resistant plants (see page 72) and make the most of winter rainfall by sealing it in with a mulch applied annually in early spring. There are many different kinds to choose from and your selection may be influenced by such factors as its appearance, whether or not it is pleasant to handle, cost and whether you want it to feed plants as well as conserve moisture. Cocoa shells and ornamental bark are attractive, pleasant to handle and make good weed suppressants, but tend to be expensive and are low in nutrients. It can be a good idea to lay a permeable membrane, available from garden centers, under bark or cocoshell mulches to suppress weeds. These membranes, however, prevent the mulch from reaching the soil, and thus conditioning it.

Garden compost and lawn clippings are free, but you may not produce enough for your needs. When using grass clippings, don't apply too thickly or heat can build up through decomposition. Animal manure is difficult to get hold of in city areas and can work out expensive, but it makes an ideal mulch as it provides nutrients and helps improve the soil structure.

During summer, high temperatures and low rainfall can send plants into a kind of dormancy and many gardens suffer from August doldrums. If there are no restrictions, one solution is to install an irrigation system. This could be something simple like a perforated hose laid between plants attached to an outside tap or a more sophisticated system of drip nozzles targeting specific plants, or even pop-up sprinklers. The best time to irrigate is early morning or in the evening so that the water has time to soak into the soil and is not evaporated by strong sunlight. It is far better to really soak the ground once a week or less than to scatter water around the borders for a few minutes a day. Frequent light watering causes roots to grow up to the surface where they are much more vulnerable to drought.

Windswept gardens often experience problems with maintaining moisture. On sunny days, wind can dry out the soil and draw water from leaves at a faster rate than the roots can soak it up. Mulches can help as can planting between more robust trees and shrubs for shelter. Avoid plants with large, thin leaves as these are particularly vulnerable and instead go for drought-resistant types.

STAKING

There are many statuesque perennials that don't require staking. But, if you live in a particularly exposed spot and have done all you can in the way of windbreaks and filters, you may still need to provide some support. The most vulnerable plants are indicated in Chapter 8. Again, be wary of overfeeding as this can make shoots too soft and plants top heavy and vulnerable to splitting or being pushed over. Some relatively short plants like *Knautia* and *Gaura* have a natural tendency to flop, but this is part of their charm and instead of staking you can let surrounding plants support them so their flowers intermingle.

Don't wait until the wind and rain have smashed a plant down. Any tying up you do then is unlikely to look natural. The trick is to push in supports when shoots are sufficiently tall to help camouflage the structure – not when they're so short that the support sticks out like a sore thumb.

By far and away the best solution is either narrow stakes available from garden centers or thin branches, such as sucker growth or whips, cut from trees and shrubs. Pushed firmly into the soil, they quickly blend in with the surrounding greenery and are barely noticeable. They generally last only for the season as they become too brittle for reuse. Another option is the use of bamboo canes or green

WINTER PROTECTION

The old-fashioned method of planting by hardiness zones has gone out the window with avid gardeners, as they always like to push the limits. In colder northern gardens, a good winter snowfall provides a wonderful blanket protecting plants from severe temperature drops. If a deep snow cover isn't guaranteed, it's necessary to mulch. A good method is to surround the plant with a chicken wire cage and fill it full of dry fallen leaves or straw. One word of warning, however: wait for the ground to freeze before mulching. If you don't, all the mice and other rodents will overwinter in this snug home, feeding on the plants you are trying to protect.

1. Lay a permeable membrane under a mulch to suppress weeds. Prepare the soil and lay the membrane on top. To plant through it, cut a cross-shaped slit and peel back the corners.

2. Plant the perennial in the hole and lay a decorative mulch on top of the membrane to conceal it.

Above: One of the best ways to support clumps of herbaceous perennials is to use natural twigs which are pushed into the ground around the emerging shoots in spring. These supports are barely visible when the plants grow.

reinforced plastic stakes and twine, to form a circle around the specimen or to create zigzag lines between plants. You can also buy a wide range of staking products, often painted green or black to blend in more readily. Simple wide mesh frames suspended over the emerging shoots are ideal for plants like peony and oriental poppy.

It's tempting to try to tie up stems sprawling out over the border edge, or to cut them hard back, especially if the lawn is suffering underneath or if the plants are making mowing a chore. Resist the urge—whatever you do won't look natural unless it was planned. If it really bothers you, lay a mowing edge of paving or brick.

Above: When perennial weeds grow up among plants it is difficult to remove them. One way is to apply a paint-on systemic weedkiller. You may need to apply more than one treatment to kill the weed.

Right: Artemisias take well from cuttings, and this is a cheap way of producing a lot of plants for ground cover.

Below: The seeding of some ornamental plants, like *Pennisetum orientale*, needs to be controlled to stop it becoming a nuisance. Cut off the flowers as they set seed.

WEED CONTROL

No matter how well you prepare the soil at planting time, no matter what mulch you use, weeds will eventually need to be dealt with. They compete with ornamentals for light, water and nutrients, and spoil the look of a display. If the weed growth is particularly dense and vigorous, it can choke a plant to death. Rather like managing pests and diseases, weed control is all about pre-empting problems and understanding something of the life cycle of the prevalent weed species.

During mild winters, you'll often get a rash of annual weed seedlings and these need to be dealt with before they begin growing in earnest and set seed. Many people spray the ground with a systemic herbicide in spring just to kill off the first flush of weed growth. Take care that you don't catch any green shoots of ornamentals as they will take the poison down inside and kill off the roots. If you garden organically, chemical sprays are of course out of the question and the only options are barriers to weed growth, and hand weeding. Hoeing can be very effective for controlling annual weeds. With perennials that have a more extensive and durable root system, chopping up the roots can lead to bigger problems as each section may grow to produce another weed. Never put perennial weed roots onto the compost heap.

Well-rotted manure or garden compost applied thickly in late winter or early spring can help to smother weeds, but equally, such mulches can contain masses of viable weed seeds, so be prepared to deal with a rash of seedlings. Relatively sterile mulches like spent mushroom compost or chipped bark may be a better option. Close planting and the use of ground cover can also help keep weeds at bay.

Most weed seeds need light to germinate and every time you disturb the soil, you bring a fresh lot of seeds to the surface. That is why you often get weeds around a newly-planted specimen. If you don't have time for a full scale weed onslaught, at least take off some of the more obvious flower heads before they set seed. And don't forget that ornamentals can become weeds if allowed to set seed.

If perennial weeds become embedded in the crown of a perennial, you have two options. One is to paint a proportion of the weed's foliage with a formulation of systemic herbicide — this may take several applications before the weed is eradicated. The second option is to dig up the rootstock and carefully disentangle the weed from the ornamental.

PESTS AND DISEASES

Face facts — you can't eradicate bugs, slugs and snails or wipe out fungal infections. They are simply part of the scheme of things and anyway, who wants to spend all their time worrying about a few chewed leaves. The best approach is to become observant and to make routine checks whether or not plants look healthy. That way you'll spot small colonies of aphids or caterpillars before they assume plague proportions. No need for sprays, just rub them off or blast them loose with the hose pipe. It's far better to look for egg clusters than to have to deal with the hatchlings. Birds and other wildlife can be a help in the battle against pests and effort should be made to encourage them into the garden. Give them predator-free places to drink and nest and provide winter feed. You could also make a pond to attract frogs and toads which eat insect pests.

Another thing to be wary of is the overuse of fertilizers. Don't think that the more you feed your garden the better it will be. The payback may be bigger blooms but if you get the balance wrong it could mean sappy shoots that are vulnerable to fungal diseases and attack by pests.

Another strategy is to carry out regular housekeeping. Remove dead foliage and blooms to lessen the risk of fungal infection and keep the base of plants clear of debris, including weeds, where pests could hide. Also get rid of daytime roosting sites for slugs and snails.

If you do need to use pest sprays, be selective. Choose a product that specifically targets the pest and does minimum harm to beneficial wildlife.

Spray before or after foraging bees are active and use only according to manufacturer's instructions. If you want to eradicate slugs and snails with bait, choose one that does not harm birds.

The same applies to various diseases. Remove affected parts of the plants and spray as directed using as inoffensive a product as possible. Some years are better or worse for fungal infections, and whether or not plants succumb may depend on factors out of your control such as extreme cold at night, drought or, alternatively, high humidity and rainfall.

SIMPLE PROPAGATION

For most perennials, the best method of propagation is division. Apart from taking cuttings, this is the only way for plants that don't come true from seed. In spring you can often buy plants from the garden center with several distinct crowns and these can be divided up to give several plants for the price of one. For large clumps lifted from the border, lay the plant on its side and, using two garden forks back to back, ease the roots apart. You can also use an old knife for division of smaller specimens.

Many perennial species and some varieties can be raised from seed as easily as hardy annuals. Either collect seed when ripe or buy it. Sow in trays or pots in the cold frame or greenhouse in spring. Some require a propagator for germination but can then be grown on without heat.

This is a good method for growing large numbers of plants for edging or ground cover. The offspring can be variable so keep only the best plants. Named clones must be propagated by division or from cuttings to ensure that an identical plant is produced.

1. Propagate iris by division, lifting clumps in the fall or immediately after flowering. Find the newest growths coming out of the main clump and cut through the thick rhizome.

2. Each division should have one or two tufts of leaves and an active growing point.

3. Trim back the leaves and replant in a sunny position with the upper half of the rhizome showing above soil level. The young divisions may need staking to prevent wind rock.

1. To grow perennials from seed, fill a clean tray with seed compost and firm lightly. Level the surface with the base of a flower pot. Pour the seed onto a piece of folded paper and gently tap the seeds out onto the compost, sowing them thinly and evenly.

2. Sieve more seed compost over the seeds to form a thin layer that just covers the seed. Label and stand the tray in a shallow bowl of water until the surface darkens.

3. Remove the tray and cover with a transparent lid, a sheet of glass or a plastic bag, supported at the corners with four sticks to keep the plastic from touching the soil. Place in a bright position out of direct sunlight, and await germination.

1. Many plants take readily from shoot tip cuttings (as shown) or basal cuttings. Treat them in the same way. Remove the lower leaves with a sharp knife, then recut the stem just below a leaf joint.

2. Fill a pot with cutting compost and firm. Pop the cuttings into holes made in the compost so the lower leaves rest on the surface. Firm and water well. Cover the pot with a plastic bag until roots appear through the drainage holes in the base of the pot.

1. Take root cuttings in winter. Lift the plant and wash away the soil. Cut 2- or 3-inch sections, angling the lower cut so you know which way up the root goes.

2. Pot up thick roots vertically into small pots or lay thinner roots in a tray; cover with a thin layer of cutting compost. Water well, then cover with plastic until new growth begins.

Left: Clumps of acanthus are made up of several separate crowns which can be divided to rejuvenate the clump and produce several new plants.

Above right: Red hot pokers produce new shoots at the base of the clumps in spring. These are ideal material to be used as basal cuttings.

Cuttings can be very easy to root using nonflowering shoot tips and side shoots in summer and fall. Some of the easiest plants to treat this way are penstemons. This method is used to insure survival of somewhat tender perennials in cold areas as well as for increasing stock. Basal cuttings taken from new shoots at the base of stems in spring can be used to propagate plants like red hot poker (*Kniphofia*) and *Aster*. Basal shoots taken early in spring can be rooted in a propagator.

For shoot tip or basal shoot cuttings, take shoots 2–3 inches long, trim off just below a leaf joint and cut off the lower leaves. Plant in compost with the lower leaves resting on the surface, water and place inside a propagator or into a large clear plastic bag. Keep in the shade and pot-on when rooted.

Some plants, including bergenia and border phlox, may be raised from root cuttings. Lift the rootstock in winter and wash off the soil by dunking in a bucket of water. Then taking a sharp knife, take off young fleshy roots and cut them up into sections. Trim off any thin fibrous roots. Place the sections in a plastic bag with some fungicide powder and give it a shake. Cut the roots into 2- or 3-inch lengths and mark the bottom of the cutting with a slanted cut. Either push vertically into pots of cutting compost so that the top of the cutting is just below the surface, or lay horizontally in seed trays, just covered with compost. Keep moist in a shaded cold frame until shoots appear, then pot up individually and grow on until large enough to plant out.

The plants described in this section represent some of the best perennials available to gardeners today. It is of course not an exhaustive list. There are so many beautiful and garden-worthy individuals, it would be impossible to fit them all in here. Each plant has had to demonstrate that it has several desirable characteristics that outweigh any faults and that, given the right circumstances, it is easy to grow and maintain.

When brand new plants come into circulation they often do so in a blaze of publicity. The way a plant is marketed can mean the difference between commercial success or failure. But if a plant is to stand the test of time, it must have more to it than mere hype. New does not always mean better. Gardeners are a discerning group and sooner or later they will embrace or reject a plant on the basis of its merit. Virtually all of the plants described in this section have undergone such a selection process and many have won awards based on trials by horticultural organizations around the world.

In these times of greater consumer awareness, people now have higher expectations of their garden plants. They must be hardier, more fragrant, bloom longer, have more than one season of interest, come in a wider

the in crowd

Whether they are old plants given a new lease of life or genuinely new varieties, these are the plants of the moment, the "in crowd." And whether you want to be fashionable or simply enjoy a great show of perennials, these are the ones to choose.

choice of colors and be resistant to pests and diseases. In reality, there are very few "perfect" plants. They nearly all have their faults and it would be churlish of us to reject them on this basis. On the other hand, it can be terribly disappointing to grow a plant only to see it curl up and die. If your

garden incorporates a substantial number of the plants detailed in this directory, you should find that your displays are attractive and reliable and that you have far fewer tedious chores related to their maintenance. Trouble-free plants means more time for enjoying your garden and for planning your next project.

Not all of the plants in this section can be described as "new". Gardening, like anything else, is subject to fashion and through history plants have gone in and out of favor. Herbaceous perennials tend to peak in popularity every 50 years or so. Such patterns are apparent from studying old nursery catalogs. Of course some have been lost forever, but it is amazing how many are resurrected once a particular plant group has a starring role once more. When a plant comes back into fashion, demands from the public for new varieties to try can cause nurserymen to search for long-forgotten specimens in gardens or historic plant collections. You sometimes hear stories of plants having been "rescued" from the brink of extinction and brought back into the trade once more.

But whether the plants you select from this section are new varieties or whether they are rediscovered old ones, they won't fail to please you.

Far left: Stachys macrantha 'Rosea', with its glossy, serrated leaves, pops up among bright green feathery fennel (Foeniculum vulgare) seedlings.

ACAENA SACCATICULPULA 'BLUE HAZE'
(New Zealand Burr)

A low-growing, evergreen ground cover plant with ferny leaves in steel-blue with a purplish cast and red stems. In fall, attractive deep red burrs appear. 'Blue Haze' is ideal for filling in gaps around the base of taller plants at the front of a border. Use it as a foil for dwarf bulbs. It needs full sun and a well-drained, not overly rich soil to bring out the color. A drought-tolerant plant, it is excellent for problem "hot spots" and containers. Zones 7–9.

ACANTHUS SPINOSUS
(Bear's Breeches)

This statuesque perennial makes a bold statement in the border, and

Agapanthus 'Anthea'

looks lovely in a scheme with purple, silver and crimson. The long, deeply-cut semi-evergreen leaves are a dark glossy green and form a large mound. Above this stand solid spires, reaching up to 5 feet, with thorny mauve bracts and protruding white flowers. Because of the everlasting quality of the bracts, the plant remains attractive well into fall. Bear's breeches looks good in a Mediterranean-style garden. It thrives in full sun and well-drained soil. In colder regions, protect the crown with mulch during the winter. Zones 5–9.

ACHILLEA (Yarrow)

One of the best known achilleas is A. filipendulina 'Gold Plate' (zones 3–9) whose flat, circular heads of yellow form a strong horizontal line at the back of the border. It needs frequent division and staking, so the spotlight has moved to some of the more easy-to-grow yarrows, especially the Galaxy Hybrids. The evergreen 'Moonshine' (zones 4–8) is popular with its dense silver-gray, feathery foliage and sulfur yellow heads produced over a long period in summer and fall. But for something with more subtle shading, try one of the creamy-yellow cultivars like 'Taygetea' (zones 3–8) or 'Hoffnung' (zones 4–8). 'Terracotta' is an apricot color, 'Salmon Beauty' is pale salmon-pink fading to cream. 'Apfelblüte', syn. 'Appleblossom' (zones 4–8), and A. millefolium 'Lilac Beauty' (zones 3–9) are soft pink and lilac-pink respectively. For a spot of red, choose 'Fanal' (zones 4–8), or 'Paprika' (zones 3–9). All are semi-evergreen and make compact plants 18–30 inches tall. Deadhead and replant every three years, and grow in full sun and well-drained soil.

ACONITUM (Monkshood)

Related to delphiniums, monkshoods produce tall spikes of purple or blue flowers. The flower stalks rarely need staking, making them an excellent substitute for delphiniums. The attractive foliage is deeply cut and appears early in the year. The foliage mounds make a good foil for bulbs.

'Sparks Variety' (zones 3–7), has deep indigo blue blossoms on 5-foot, branching stems. A. carmichaelii 'Arendsii' (zones 3–7), is similar but with single spires coming into bloom slightly later. The flowers of Aconitum x cammarum 'Bicolor' (zones 3–7), look as though they have been painted in watercolors and are white with blue staining. For a change from the blues try A. napellus vulgare 'Carneum' (zones 5–8), a pale flesh pink, or the pure white A. 'Ivorine' (zones 5–8), that often continues blooming for months.

Grow monkshood in either full sun or light shade in rich, moisture-retentive soil. Cut out the main flower spike as it fades to make way for fresh new laterals. Lift and divide every three or four years for best flowering performance. Monkshood is highly toxic if eaten.

AGAPANTHUS
(Blue African Lily)

Add a touch of the tropics to your late summer border with this sculptural plant. Above a clump of strap-shaped leaves, smooth stems bear large, rounded heads of tubular, flared blooms. Agapanthus looks magnificent spilling out over the border edge, especially onto light-colored paving or gravel. These plants also make great container specimens.

There's now a wide range of frost-hardy cultivars to choose from, including the 'Headbourne Hybrids' which are hardy from zones 6–9. Most agapanthus flower in shades of blue, although there are some white varieties such as 'Bressingham White' (zones 7–10). Depending on the variety, they flower in mid- to late summer or fall. Plant heights range from the very tall (such as 'Blue Giant' which reaches 3–4 feet) to the dwarf such as 'Lilliput' and 'Peter Pan' which are 12–18 inches tall. As a rule of thumb, the narrower the leaf, the hardier the cultivar. Deciduous ones also are hardier than evergreens, but even the cold-tolerant agapanthus are not reliably hardy. In very cold regions, mulch the crowns in winter to protect them. Grow in full sun on deep, well-cultivated soil.

AJUGA REPTANS
(Carpet Bugleweed)

Bugles are semi-evergreen, creeping plants with rounded leaves, ideal as fillers for a mixed border. There are several colored-leaf varieties, such as Ajuga reptans 'Burgundy Glow', with leaves marbled in shades of pink and white that look lovely with silvers and pastel blues. 'Atropurpurea' has deep bronze-purple foliage but the best purple is 'Braunherz'. Its evergreen leaves make it a useful backdrop for bulbs in spring. Rich blue flower spikes appear from April to May. 'Catlin's Giant' and 'Jungle Beauty' have much larger bronze leaves and blue flowers. Grow colored-leaf types in sun or light shade. 'Variegata' retains its color better than others in shade. Avoid dry sites which can cause mildew. Zones 3–9.

ALCHEMILLA MOLLIS
(Lady's Mantle)

The soft green leaves of this beautiful plant are rounded in outline with a scalloped edge and appear faintly pleated. They form low mounds and after rain the beads of water trapped on the leaf hairs sparkle magically. In early summer, a froth of tiny lime green flowers appears, making a foil for just about any flower color. When the flowers fade, cut the whole plant back with sheers or a weed wacker to encourage fresh new growth which will last through fall. Feed and water at the same time. Grow in sun or part shade and in any soil other than waterlogged. Its only vice is its propensity to seed around, but it is a lovely way to soften the edge of a path. Zones 4–7.

Alchemilla mollis

ALLIUM
(Ornamental Onion)

Strictly speaking these plants are bulbs, but they are used in the mixed border much like perennials. They have become fashionable in recent years. The drumstick-like flower heads, which come mostly in shades of purple, make these excellent plants for weaving through a mixed border. As they flower between May and June, they make a useful link between spring and summer flowers. The perfect, globe-shaped blooms are very distinctive, rising up on smooth, leafless stems. The exquisite seed heads are long lasting, eventually turning a pale biscuit color.

Among the best of the taller types at 3 feet are A. hollandicum (zones 4–10) and the form 'Purple Sensation' (zones 4–9), A. giganteum (zones 6–10) and A. rosenbachianum (zones 4–10). For the front of a border, try A. christophii (zones 5–8), with starry blooms arranged in large, but airy heads perched on short stems, and also A. schubertii (zones 4–10), which has amazing seed heads reminiscent of an exploding firework. Both flower slightly later in June or July. Allium sphaerocephalon (zones 4–10), also flowers at this time, but has many smaller, egg-shaped heads in deep reddish purple and forms handsome spreading clumps up to about 24 inches high.

They like plenty of moisture during winter and spring when starting into growth, but need a dry summer to prevent the dormant bulbs rotting. One technique to insure a dry summer environment for allium is to plant them near deciduous shrubs and perennials. These actively-growing plants will soak up most moisture before it affects the summer-dormant bulbs. Plant bulbs in September or October, covering with three to four times their own depth in soil. Only lift and divide the clumps when flowering begins to fall off.

ANEMONE
(Japanese Anemone)

The hybrids of Anemone x hybrida, together with selections of the very similar Anemone hupehensis, are some of the most useful plants for the late summer and fall garden. None needs staking, although some reach up to 5 feet, and they are generally carefree, resenting root disturbance. Japanese anemones can verge on invasive if they like the conditions, so let them loose in an established shrub border where they will be able to spread themselves around.

Anemone x hybrida

All Japanese anemone cultivars make basal clumps of handsome vine-like leaves above which wiry branched stems carry the spherical buds and dish-shaped flowers. One of the loveliest is 'Honorine Jobert', a classic, pure white cultivar with large blooms marked at the center with a boss of golden stamens. For a shorter white-flowering variety, choose 'Luise Uhink' or the semi-double 'Whirlwind'. Most of the other cultivars come in shades of cool pink. 'September Charm' is single, while 'Königin Charlotte' is a reliable semi-double. 'Prinz Heinrich' is a deep pink shade and 'Bressingham Glow' deeper still. With the exception of 'Honorine Jobert', all these reach up to 2–3 feet or slightly taller.

Japanese anemones tolerate a range of conditions, but grow best in humus-rich, well-drained soils. They like a sunny spot, but will do well in moderate shade. Zones 4–8.

Allium giganteum

ANGELICA ARCHANGELICA (Archangel)

The herb angelica is becoming more and more fashionable because of its bold shape and sculptural nature, qualities now sought after in contemporary garden design.

When grown as a single specimen, angelica makes a strong focal point in the late summer border. It is a short-lived perennial or biennial which makes a basal clump of deeply-divided leaves and then, in its flowering year, sends up thick branching stems some 6–8 feet high topped with greenish-white, umbrella-like flower heads. If the seedheads are not removed, the plant will die, but since these are extremely ornamental, most gardeners leave them, at least until the plant has had a chance to self-seed. Transplant the resultant seedlings to a suitable site before they get too large as they are tap-rooted and resent disturbance. Angelica will be happy in sun or shade, and likes a well-drained soil. Zones 4–9.

ANTHEMIS TINCTORIA (Golden Marguerite)

Apart from the huge amount of flowers produced, the good thing about these daisy-flowered perennials is the subtle range of yellows available, which work beautifully with soft blues and purples. The palest of them and first to flower between May and July is 'Sauce Hollandaise' with yellow buds opening to cream with yellow centers. Then come the cool lemon 'E.C.Buxton' and creamy yellow 'Wargrave Variety', both of which bloom for many weeks in the summer. All are evergreen, and make spreading domes of ferny foliage over which many long-stemmed daisies appear. 'E.C. Buxton' is the most compact at only 12–20 inches, the others are taller at 3 feet and usually need stakes for support. Grow in full sun and in well-drained soil. Lift and divide the clumps every few years. Shear the plant when the flowers fade to encourage lusher leaves and more flowers. Zones 3–7.

Anthemis tinctoria 'Sauce Hollandaise'

Artemisia 'Powis Castle'

ARMERIA MARITIMA
(Sea Pink, Thrift)

Thrift is a wild plant that grows on coastal cliffs, but it has made a very successful transition into gardens. It forms a neat grassy evergreen hummock 4x6 inches with rounded clear pink flower heads growing on wiry, unbranched stems from late spring to summer. 'Alba' is a good white flowering cultivar. 'Düsseldorfer Stolz' has larger flowers on shorter stems in deep reddish pink and reaches up to 6 inches. 'Vindictive', a deep rose-pink, is very long-flowered from late spring to midsummer and is slightly taller. The brightest and biggest of them all is 'Bees Ruby', a vivid pink thrift measuring 12x12 inches. All require a sunny well-drained site. Zones 3–9.

ARTEMISIA

There are a large number of these striking silver-leaved plants to choose from, most of which thrive in hot spots on dry, relatively poor soil. Some of the tougher evergreens like 'Powis Castle' (zones 7–9), 3x4 feet, and the aromatic wormwood Artemisia absinthium 'Lambrook Silver' (zones 4–8), 30 inches, have shimmering feathery leaves. Others, including forms of Artemisia stelleriana (zones 3–7) have lacy evergreen foliage that looks as though it's been cut from white felt. The foliage of A. alba 'Canescens', (zones 4–8), 18x12 inches, is just like fine, silver-white wispy curls. The leaves of A. ludoviciana (zones 4–9), 4x2 feet, and A. l. 'Silver Queen', 3x2 feet, are gray-white and willow like. These plants are wonderful for weaving through the summer border. The one exception to the silver foliage is

Artemisia lactiflora, (zones 5–8), 6x2 feet, whose upright stems are clothed in deeply-cut green leaves and topped with creamy-white flower plumes. These tall border perennials like a moisture-retentive, fertile soil. Shrubby types like 'Powis Castle' can be cut back in late spring to promote growth of bushy young foliage.

ARUM ITALICUM
ITALICUM 'MARMORATUM'
(Lords and Ladies)

Don't let the long latin name put you off. This is a beautiful foliage plant for semi-shade and can light up the winter garden. The arrow-shaped leaves, which appear in late fall, are heavily veined and marbled palest gray-green and cream. In early summer when the foliage has died down completely, white flowers (technically "spathes") appear, but these are insignificant compared with the spikes of gleaming orange-red berries that follow in late summer. This plant grows up to 12 inches in height. Plant in moisture-retentive but well-drained soil. Take care as this plant is highly poisonous if eaten. Zones 6–9.

ARUNCUS DIOICUS
(Goat's Beard)

It looks like it should be a bog plant, with it's lush leafiness and creamy-white plumes, but goat's beard is happy in an ordinary bed, and even will tolerate the odd dry spell. However, it grows best on rich, moisture-retentive ground in light shade. The 4-foot mound of large fern-like leaves is impressive in it's own right, but the midsummer flower stems increase the height to 6–7 feet.

There are male and female forms, although these are not very often distinguished in nurseries. The males have the most showy flowers, but the females have interesting seedheads and produce offspring with ease. Goat's beard makes an impressive specimen or background plant for a large border or woodland garden. If you are short on space, there is the charming 'Kneiffii' with finely-dissected leaves, which only grows to 3 feet in height. Zones 3–7.

ASPLENIUM
(Hart's Tongue Fern)

The hart's tongue is a handsome, evergreen fern that makes a crown of undulating strap-like fronds. It's a good one to try if you have a lime-rich soil. In the wild you sometimes see it colonizing old walls. Although drought tolerant, it grows larger and more luxuriantly on deep, moisture-retentive, well-drained soil in a shady site. Tidy up the plants in spring by removing the old, dead fronds. Grows up to 22x14 inches. Zones 6–8.

ASTELIA CHATHAMICA

This evergreen perennial from New Zealand makes an upright clump of sword-like leaves in striking metallic-silver, each with a stunning white-felted underside. With its subtropical looks, it makes a wonderful specimen for a large pot on the patio. Astelia likes a moist, acidic loamy soil and, especially during the summer months, should not go short of water. Insignificant flowers may appear, followed by orange berries if fertilized by another plant. Clumps grow up to 5x8 feet. Zones 8–9.

ASTER (Michaelmas Daisy)

If you're going to grow just one, and there are hundreds, pick the superlative Aster x frikartii 'Mönch' (zones 5–8), at 30x18 inches. The common Michaelmas daisy suffers from mildew and wilt and usually needs staking. Many dwarf cultivars with large flowers have been developed, but they lack the grace of the more old-fashioned kinds. 'Mönch' has large, single daisy-like flowers in a gentle lavender blue that goes with absolutely everything. The flowers last well and rarely need to be staked.

A group of easy-care fall-flowering asters that are beginning to get more attention now are ones producing a profusion of tiny blooms on much branched stems with needle-like foliage. These include compact forms of Aster ericoides, (zones 5–8), at 3 feet tall, such as 'Blue Star' (pale blue), 'Esther' (pink), 'Golden Spray' (pink-tinged white flower heads with golden yellow disk florets), and 'White Heather' (white). Also try A. lateriflorus 'Horizontalis' (zones 4–8), whose fall foliage is purple tinged, making a lovely foil for the pale lilac flowers. It grows to 2 feet tall. Grow asters on moist, fertile, well-drained soil in full sun or very light shade.

ASTILBE

Astilbes can be best appreciated when planted in swathes alongside water. They thrive in boggy conditions, but will also grow in a normal border provided the soil is moisture-retentive, or mulched with organic matter, and lightly shaded. The feathery flower plumes bloom mostly in the summer. They come in a wide range of colors

from white through every shade of pink, purple and red. Some, such as 'Fanal' (zones 4–9), have red or bronze foliage. The seedheads turn dark chestnut brown and remain attractive until spring, when they should be removed as part of the general spring cleaning. In some cultivars the flower heads form dense upright spikes, but the majority produce delicate open sprays or fluffy plumes. Plants are best left undisturbed and will spread. Good tall cultivars at 3 feet include pinks such as 'Erica' (zones 5–8) and 'Bressingham Beauty' (zones 4–8), reds such as 'Glut', and the brighter 'Feuer' (both zones 5–8), and the clear lilac-pink 'Amethyst' and slightly shorter 'Hyazinth' (both zones 4–8). Next come plants at 18–24 inches, such as the crimson 'Fanal', the white 'Deutschland' (both zones 4–9), 'Irrlicht' (zones 4–9), 'Snowdrift' (zones 5–8), and clear pink 'Rheinland'

(zones 4–8). For the front of border, try 'Bronce Elegans', with pink-salmon plumes and bronzy leaves or 'Sprite' in shell pink (both zones 4–8). The late-flowering A. chinensis 'Pumila' (zones 4–8), at 18x24 inches, produces pale mauve-pink blooms over a ground-covering mat of leaves.

ASTILBOIDES TABULARIS

This highly architectural plant is rather like a smaller, more refined version of the giant Gunnera, often seen growing by lakes in parks. Astilboides is also a bog garden plant and in good conditions, the circular, sharply-lobed leaves can reach 3 feet across. With the stalks coming into the center of the leaf, they are reminiscent of umbrellas. As well as the magnificent leaves, astilboides produces 5-foot high stems of creamy-white flowers. Grow in a spot sheltered from wind. Zones 5–7.

Aruncus dioicus

Astrantia major involucrata 'Shaggy'

ASTRANTIA (Masterwort)

The masterworts are subtle in their overall effect, but each flower head is like an old-fashioned posy. The species that most of the varieties and cultivars come from is greater masterwort, Astrantia major (zones 4–7), flowering in early and midsummer. It has green-white, pink-tinged blooms and deeply lobed, tooth-edged foliage and grows to 24x18 inches. 'Claret', 'Hadspen Blood', 'Ruby Wedding' and rubra all have deep purplish-red blooms while A. major rosea is a soft dusky pink. 'Shaggy' has larger, somewhat untidy blooms in white-tipped green. For cream and yellow-edged foliage, try 'Sunningdale Variegated'. A. maxima (zones 5–8), has particularly attractive flowers in a pretty clear rose pink.

The masterworts should be grown in a well-drained, humus-rich soil. If they are given moisture they will grow happily in a full sun position and will tolerate drier conditions when grown in partial shade.

ATHYRIUM FILIX-FEMINA (Lady Fern)

The highly-dissected fronds of the lady fern are a light, fresh green. This lovely fern combines beautifully with other shade plants that have broad leaves. As well as shade, it needs a moisture-retentive soil with plenty of humus and prefers slightly acidic conditions. It grows to 20x12 inches. Zones 4–9.

BALLOTA

Ballota 'All Hallow's Green' (zones 7–9) is a stylish member of the sage family with soft, lime green foliage which acts as a foil for any other color in a sunny border. The leaves are rounded, and the upright shoots are topped with whorls of pale green flowers. At 12x18 inches, it makes an ideal plant for the front of a border. B. pseudodictamnus (zones 7–9) is a little bit larger. Its leaves have a woolly coating, making them appear more gray tinged. Grow in well-drained but moisture-retentive soil in full sun. Zones 7–9.

BAPTISIA AUSTRALIS (False Indigo)

Baptisia flowers in early summer when the clumps of new foliage are a lovely blue-green. It sends up loose flower heads of deep, violet blue with orange anthers. The light green leaves remain attractive through to the fall when the whole plant turns black with frost. Once planted, false indigo is best left undisturbed. It thrives in full sun on deep, well-cultivated soil on the acid side of neutral. Stake plants growing in windy gardens. It grows to 24x36 inches. Zones 3–9.

BERGENIA
(Elephant's Ears)

With spreading clumps of large, rounded, glossy evergreen leaves, bergenias make a dramatic contrast to more upright plants. In spring, tight heads of waxy, bell-shaped blooms appear which provide a useful source of nectar for early bumble bees. Breeders have extended the flower color range to include whites through various pinks and purples to deep red. Dwarf cultivars (to 10 inches) include the pale pink 'Baby Doll' and pinkish-red 'Wintermärchen' (both zones 4–8), whose pointed leaves glow red in winter. Among larger-leaved plants (18x18 inches), good whites include 'Bressingham White' and 'Beethoven' (both zones 4–8) and 'Silberlicht' (zones 3–8). Deep pinks include 'Abendglut' (zones 3–8), with good red winter coloring, 'Bressingham Ruby' and 'Morgenröte' (both zones 3–8). 'Bressingham Salmon' (zones 4–8) is an unusual salmon-pink and 'Sunningdale' (zones 3–8) is rosy pink on rich red stems with bronze-tinted leaves in winter. The magenta B. cordifolia 'Purpurea', and pink B. purpurascens (both zones 3–8) have beet-red winter coloring.

Clumps should be lifted and divided every few years. Cut the dead flower heads out at the base and pull off foliage when it fades. Bergenias will perform best in full sun on a fertile, moisture-retentive soil, although they will tolerate dry shade.

BRUNNERA MACROPHYLLA

This relative of the forget-me-not is a first-rate ground cover plant which produces a mass of large, roughly heart-shaped leaves. There are two variegated varieties, 'Dawson's White' and 'Hadspen Cream', but these have insufficient vigor for ground cover. In spring, the starry, light blue flowers seem to float on wiry stems above the newly-expanded foliage. Grow in dappled shade unless plentiful moisture is available. The variegated cultivars are best in a sheltered, shady position on moisture-retentive soil. Brunnera grows to 20 inches high. Zones 3–7.

CALAMINTHA (Calamint)

The lesser calamints, Calamintha nepeta and C. n. nepeta (syn. C. nepetoides) are aromatic herbs with a long season of flowering from late summer into fall. The plants form low hummocks of small, mint-scented leaves over which wiry stems bear clouds of tiny pale mauve-blue flowers which the bees find irresistible. It self-seeds quite readily. Grow in full sun on free-draining soil and cut the flower stems back to ground level before new growth begins in spring. Up to 18x18 inches. Zones 5–9.

CAMPANULA (Bellflower)

This is a very large genus with plants ranging from tiny alpines to rampant ground cover, and tall summer border perennials that send up erect flower stems from an evergreen clump of leaves. The often blue, bell-shaped flowers are the main recognition feature of the bellflowers. There are many double-flowered cultivars that are old-fashioned in appearance. Two of the more unusual border species include the elegant Campanula alliariifolia, ivory bells (zones 3–7), with narrow spires of long, creamy-white hanging bells, and the spreading C. takesimana (zones 5–8), whose large, tubular bells are a pale lavender, speckled maroon inside (both 20x24 inches).

A common sight in cottage gardens is the charming peach-leaved bellflower, C. persicifolia (zones 3–8), growing to 36 inches, which is at it's flowering peak from early to midsummer, with loose, cup-shaped bells in light lavender. 'Alba' is a white form and both self-sow freely. Another self-seeder and similar in appearance is C. latiloba (zones 4–8), and its white form 'Alba'. C. lactiflora (zones 4–8), is taller and in windy sites, plants usually need staking, especially the larger forms like the violet-blue 'Prichard's Variety'. The large, dome-shaped flower heads last from summer until early fall and consist of many lilac-blue bells (or lilac-pink in the case of 'Loddon Anna'). C. poscharskyana, the Dalmatian bellflower (zones 4–7), makes good spreading ground cover, growing to about 6 inches tall and around 24 inches wide.

Most border bellflowers are easy to grow, preferring a fertile, moisture-retentive soil in a sunny site, although Campanula alliariifolia, C. poschar-skyana, and C. persicifolia all do well in a semi-shaded site.

Campanula lactiflora 'Pritchard's Variety'

Carex elata 'Aurea'

CAREX
(Ornamental Sedge)

Like grasses, ornamental sedges are very much in vogue. Most are grown mainly for their handsome, evergreen foliage. They come in a bewildering range of size, color and variegation and are easy to grow in sun or shade, but do best on moisture-retentive, humus-rich or peaty soil.

One sedge grown for its flowers is the pendulous or weeping sedge (Carex pendula, zones 5–9). This plant would suit a woodland border or, better still, a wild waterside planting, where the long arching stems could display their fox-tail flowers to best advantage. Flowering late spring and early summer, it reaches 3–4 feet and produces spreading clumps of dark green, upright, evergreen foliage.

The leatherleaf sedge grass (C. buchananii, zones 6–9), which grows up to 24 inches high, and the bronze form of C. comans (zones 7–9) 12x36 inches, make arching hummocks of narrow pinkish-brown foliage which in fall and winter has an orange glow about it. Try either of them in a sunny border, combined with blue and silver foliage and flowers.

Another curious cultivar for a sunny border is the aptly-named 'Frosted Curls' (zones 7–9). The very narrow leaves are a whitish-green and the tips lightly curled to magical effect. It grows to 12x 24 inches.

The Japanese sedge grass (Carex oshimensis, zones 6–9) makes low arching hummocks of bright gold and green striped evergreen leaves.

Bowles' golden sedge (C. elata 'Aurea', zones 5–9) is a like a shaft of sunlight. It will do best in a moist shady flower border. The arching leaves are a fresh, glowing yellow. It forms clumps 24x36 inches.

CENTRANTHUS RUBER
(Red Valerian)

One of the main features of this plant is its long flowering period, right through summer. The domed dusky-pink flower heads consist of many tiny blooms that are rich in nectar and attract butterflies and hawk moths. The plants are drought resistant. In the wild, red valerian can be found clinging to cliffs around the coast, and growing in the crumbling mortar of old walls. As well as the usual pink, you sometimes see deep crimson red and pure white varieties growing alongside each other. These are C. ruber 'Coccineus' and C. r. 'Albus'. These are easy plants to grow given full sun and a well-drained soil, especially one that is limey, and they will seed freely in favorable conditions. Cut back the plants after the first flush of flowers to improve habit and encourage further blooms. Plants grow to 24 inches high. Zones 5–8.

CERATOSTIGMA
WILLMOTTIANUM
(Hardy or Chinese Plumbago)

This vivid blue-flowered gem is technically a subshrub, but in cold climates it dies down to ground level just like a herbaceous plant. Flowering in late summer and fall, it makes a perfect partner for all the fall tints that abound at that time. The small leaves covering the wiry stems become red-tinted in the fall, adding to the effect. It forms mounds 36x36 inches. Grow in a sunny, well-drained position and cut down the dead stems in spring before the new growth commences. Zones 6–9.

CERINTHE MAJOR
'PURPURASCENS'
(Honeywort, Wax Flower)

This slightly tender, evergreen plant is a member of the borage family that has brought so many wonderful blue-flowered plants into the garden. Cerinthe is quite simply a symphony in blue. Even the fleshy leaves that spiral up the stem are blue tinged, and toward the tip there are sea-blue bracts surmounting nodding clusters of purple-blue bell flowers. The flowers are rich in nectar and popular with bees. It grows to 18 inches tall. Grow

Cimicifuga racemosa

CIMICIFUGA (Bugbane)

These elegant, late-flowering plants with deeply-cut leaves and elegant, white, bottlebrush flowers make good back-of-the-border specimens for a moist, shady site. On drier soils, try the less demanding black snakeroot (C. racemosa, zones 3–8). It flowers earliest and continues to throw up new shoots throughout the summer. Mulch heavily with organic matter to conserve moisture. It grows to 6–7 feet with a spread of only 20 inches.

C. simplex cultivars (zones 4–8) flower in fall with arching, wand-like flowers. The cultivar 'White Pearl' is paler overall with light green leaves, white flowers and lime-green seed-heads. 'Elstead' has mahogany stems and brown buds, which make a good contrast with the creamy flowers. The Atropurpurea Group has purple-tinted foliage, which can be darker or lighter depending on the plant. 'Brunette' is a particularly good dark-leaved selection. All grow to 4 feet tall. Cimicifuga has recently been reclassified as Actaea, but it will be some time before the new name is generally used.

CHAEROPHYLLUM HIRSUTUM 'ROSEUM' (Pink Cow Parsley)

With its ferny foliage and domed, lilac-pink umbels of flowers, this unusual and enchanting perennial has much to offer the gardener. It blooms in late spring and early summer, then often goes on to produce a second floral crop later in the summer. It is extremely versatile and will grow happily in sun or partial shade in ordinary border conditions, although it is happiest on moisture-retentive ground. This very pretty cow parsley look-alike looks wonderful in both formal situations and in wild or woodland gardens. Divide the clumps every few years to keep plants flowering well. Protect young plants from slug and snail attacks. It grows to form clumps 18x18 inches. Zones 6–9.

in a warm, sheltered spot on free-draining soil and provide winter protection in exposed areas. If you have difficulty locating plants, it is available from seed merchants. Zones 8–10.

CONVOLVULUS SABATIUS

This bindweed cousin puts on a non-stop display of lilac-blue blooms from summer well into the fall. It is quick growing and sends out long creeping stems with small grayish-green ever-green leaves. Deeper blue shades are available. Although slightly tender in some areas, it can be overwintered in many gardens simply by insulating the roots. In cold areas, grow in pots and bring inside over winter. Height about 6 inches, spread may be in excess of 20 inches. Zones 8–9.

Crocosmia 'Jupiter'

COREOPSIS VERTICILLATA 'MOONBEAM'

Most yellow-flowered coreopsis are rather brash and brassy but the starry flowers of 'Moonbeam', produced from early summer until the fall, are a lovely soft yellow, which is enhanced by the fine, ferny bronze foliage. The plants are short lived so it's wise to take stem cuttings during the summer as a precaution. Grow in full sun on well-drained soil. The hummocks reach 24x18 inches. Zones 4–9.

CORTADERIA SELLOANA 'AUREOLINEATA' (Variegated Pampas Grass)

The fluffy white plumes of Pampas grass have become something of a cliché, but this yellow-variegated form is different in character. The 4-foot high arching mound of leaves gleams brightly in the winter sunshine, and during the growing season, they form an attractive foil for broad-leaved plants and flowers. A few flower plumes are produced in the fall. Grow in a sunny, open position on fertile, well-drained soil. In spring pull off any dead leaves that have accumulated at the base, wearing thick gloves to protect your hands. Zones 7–10.

CORYDALIS

For a long time, the only corydalis around was the yellow Corydalis lutea (zones 5–8). This ferny-leaved plant colonizes walls and paths in shady areas, producing a non-stop supply of airy yellow flower sprays between spring and the fall. It grows to 8 inches. The creamy-flowered C. ochroleuca (zones 6–8) behaves in a similar way. Nowadays, even garden centers sell C. flexuosa (zones 6–8) with its intense blue flowers. Look for 'Père David' with blue-green leaves, 'China Blue' with bronzy leaves and the aptly-named 'Purple Leaf'. Unlike some of the other species, these herbaceous plants are relatively easy to grow, but won't tolerate clay soils. They like a loose, open-textured soil with plenty of leafmold or moss peat. They produce leaves in the fall and grow slowly through winter to flower in spring or early summer. The clumps reach 12x12 inches.

CRAMBE CORDIFOLIA

In early summer, this plant is nothing short of spectacular – a giant cloud of tiny white blooms. The stems are self-supporting and plants need very little maintenance. The only drawback is that it dies away to leave a gap so you need to anticipate this and grow tall, late-flowering annuals in the foreground as camouflage. Grow in full sun on well-drained soil toward the back of the border. It reaches 8 feet in height and 5 feet across while in flower. Zones 6–9.

CRAMBE MARITIMA
(Sea Kale)

In the past, sea kale was chiefly grown as a vegetable, but today it is highly prized as a foliage plant for hot, sunny borders and gravel gardens. As its common name suggests, it is highly tolerant of salt-laden sea air. The handsome blue-green leaves, deeply lobed and notched, can reach up to 24 inches in length. They make a large clump above which, in early summer, substantial heads of white flowers appear. 30x36 inches. Zones 6–9.

CROCOSMIA (Montbretia)

With their vibrant red, orange or yellow blooms and strong architectural qualities, crocosmias have a distinctly modern feel and, flowering in late summer, they can give new life to a flagging border display.

The sprays of trumpet-shaped blooms are either arching or held horizontally. They fade gracefully, without the need for deadheading. Some have two-tone blooms, such as 'Jackanapes' which has alternating dark orange and yellow petals or 'Emily McKenzie' whose orange blooms have distinctive mahogany red throat markings.

Foliage varies from arching to stiff, upright blades. That of the flame-red 'Lucifer' is most striking: sword-shaped leaves arranged in fans up to 3 feet in height. Most are 18–36 inches tall.

Crocosmias like a fertile, moisture-retentive, well-drained soil in a sunny border. Avoid clay, and if your soil is light and sandy, dig in organic matter before planting. The large-flowered cultivars are harder to please than the smaller-flowering varieties, demanding a rich, deep loam and an abundance of summer moisture. Give plants a sheltered site in cold areas. Water in dry spells and mulch heavily. Cultivars with bronze-tinted foliage like 'Solfaterre' may suffer from scorching and do best sheltered from midday sun. Divide clumps every three or four years to maintain flowering performance. Zones 6–9.

CYNARA CARDUNCULUS
(Cardoon)

Like sea kale, the cardoon was once principally grown as a vegetable, but it makes a striking focal point in late summer with its tower of silver-gray foliage and stems topped by large artichoke-like flower heads that open to purple or blue. The leaves are spectacularly large and jagged. They appear very early and rapidly build up into a large silvery mound. Grow in a hot sunny spot with well-drained soil, preferably sheltered from wind. It reaches 6x3 feet. Zones 7–9.

DARMERA PELTATA
(Umbrella Plant)

This bog plant gives a jungle-feel to a garden. The broadly spherical, lobed and notched leaves are 12 inches or more across and make a luxuriant canopy in summer. In early spring, the plant looks like an alien creature with its naked flower stems rising up from the creeping rhizome, bearing clusters

of pale pink blooms. These are rather vulnerable to frost so may need protection. Grow in sun or partial shade in deep, constantly moist soil. Plants grow to 4 feet high. Zones 5–9.

DESCHAMPSIA
(Tufted Hair Grass)

The shimmering, cloud-like flower heads of tufted hair grass appear in summer, with the stems retaining their fragile beauty through till early winter. All produce small, dense tussocks of narrow evergreen leaves that are completely dwarfed at flowering time. The best known cultivars are D. cespitosa 'Bronzeschleier' (also known as 'Bronze Veil') which opens silvery green and gradually turns to bronze (4 feet); 'Goldschleier' ('Golden Veil') that turns bright yellow with age (4 feet) and 'Goldtau' ('Golden Dew') that begins a silvery-brown and slowly

Cynara cardunculus

Diascia 'Coral Belle'

turns to gold (30 inches). D. flexuosa (wavy hair grass, zones 4–9) is a diminutive version only reaching 18 inches. 'Tatra Gold' has yellowish-green leaves and contrasting reddish-brown flowers in early and midsummer. These beautiful grasses all prefer moisture-retentive, acidic soil and some shade. Zones 5–9.

DIASCIA

From a creeping, evergreen mat of tiny leaves, wiry stems carry a profusion of shell-shaped blooms ranging from salmon and apricot, such as Diascia barberae 'Blackthorn Apricot' and D. 'Salmon Supreme' (both zones 8–9); through to lilac-pink, such as 'Twinkle'. The hardiest of the smaller species and cultivars are the deep pink 'Ruby Field' (zones 8–9) and paler D. vigilis (zones 7–9). 'Rupert Lambert' (zones 8–9) is also pink. D. vigilis is the most vigorous, but most reach 18 inches in height and at least

16 inches across. The flowering season lasts from summer through till the frosts, provided the spent stems are removed after each main flush of flowers. D. rigescens (zones 7–9) is somewhat different in character with upright dense spikes of large pale pink flowers.

DICENTRA
(Bleeding Heart)

These dainty woodlanders have arching sprays of heart-shaped flowers in all shades of pink, as well as white, and beautiful ferny foliage, sometimes tinged blue or gray. The low-growing cultivars, derived mainly from D. formosa (zones 4–8) are very versatile. Flowering in late spring, they can be grown under trees and shrubs. Given cool, shady conditions on humus-rich, moisture-retentive soil, flowering may continue well into the summer.

For white flowers, choose 'Silver Smith' or D. eximia 'Snowdrift' (zones 4–8) with gray-tinged leaves. For pale pink flowers and blue-gray leaves, choose 'Stuart Boothman' (zones 3–9), 'Langtrees' (zones 4–8), or the vigorous carpeting D. formosa oregona. 'Spring Morning' (zones 3–9), is a lovely pale pink and among the deeper pinks are 'Luxuriant' and 'Bountiful' (both zones 4–8). 'Adrian Bloom' (zones 4–8), with gray-tinged leaves and 'Bacchanal' (zones 3–9) are two excellent reds. The cultivars all grow to around 10x8 inches.

Rosy-pink D. spectabilis (zones 3–9) is a very old garden plant, and at 24x18 inches is larger. 'Alba' is a white form. The only downside is that it dies down by midsummer, leaving a hole that may need camouflaging.

DICTAMNUS ALBUS
(Burning Bush)

Dictamnus are aromatic plants. The common name comes from the fact that on hot days you can ignite the star-shaped seed pods, which are rich in volatile oils, without harming the plant. That party trick aside, the chief reason for growing this bushy, early summer-flowering perennial is the upright spikes of white, "butterfly" flowers with long stamens. The leathery, green leaflets smell vaguely of lemons when crushed. Grow in full sun or light shade on fertile well-drained soil and leave undisturbed. It grows to 36 inches high. Zones 3–8.

DIERAMA PULCHERRIMUM
(Angel's Fishing Rod)

With long, arching flower stems bearing hanging bells of deep rose pink, this is one of the most graceful of all the late summer plants. The grassy, evergreen leaves form clumps. Grown next to water, the effect is distinctly oriental. Like so many South African plants, these bulbs prefer a soil that doesn't dry out in summer. Choose a warm, sunny position and plant in spring to give it a chance to establish properly before the winter. It is 5 feet tall in flower. Zones 8–10.

DORONICUM
(Leopard's Bane)

These old garden plants have a rather modern feel with their simple heart-shaped leaves and large single daisies (there are doubles but they don't have the same charm). Most flower in late spring and the bright leaves and yellow flowers are perfect for lighting up a shady spot. The best ones for general

Dierama pulcherrimum

garden use are the shorter hybrids and cultivars such as D. x excelsum 'Harpur Crewe' (24 inches) and D. 'Miss Mason', a compact plant suitable for the front of a mixed border (18x24 inches). D. pardalianches has a spreading rootstock (36x24 inches) and can be naturalized in thin grass. Grow these plants in full sun or shade on well-drained soil. Deadhead them regularly to encourage repeat flowering through into midsummer. Lift and divide the clumps every three or four years. Zones 4–8.

DRYOPTERIS
(Buckler Fern)

The male fern, Dryopteris filix-mas (zones 4–8), is one of the easiest hardy ferns to cultivate, growing in any soil that is not waterlogged and even tolerating a fair degree of drought. In spring, the shuttlecock of feathery fronds opens out and plants can attain anything up to 3 feet in height and spread. They make impressive specimens for pots and other containers. The male fern can be grown in sun provided it has enough moisture, but in drier areas it does need some shade. It is evergreen in mild gardens. There are numerous attractive forms with heavily dissected and intricately-wrought foliage. The golden male fern (D. affinis, zones 6–8), is similar in size and shape to the male fern.

For a smaller specimen, try the evergreen copper shield fern (Dryopteris erythrosora, zones 6–9). Its new young fronds are tinted an attractive pinkish-brown. Grow in shade and shelter on a moist, humus-rich soil. 16x12 inches.

Echinops bannaticus

ECHINACEA PURPUREA (Coneflower)

The coneflower produces substantial daisy-like blooms, each with a large central cone of glowing ginger-brown. These plants are very popular with bees and butterflies. The straight species has wide, rich pink petals but in the superior cultivar 'Robert Bloom', the color is intensified to a much richer mauve-crimson. 'Magnus' has large single or semi-double flowers in a deep purple. The white cultivars include 'White Swan' and 'White Lustre'. Coneflowers need moisture-retentive, humus-rich soil and grow best in full sun. They will not tolerate water logging, especially during the winter months. 3–4 feet tall. Zones 3–9.

ECHINOPS (Globe Thistle)

The flower heads of this statuesque perennial are spiny globes of soft blue, carried at the tips of branching stems. They flower from midsummer to early fall and make perfect background plants for other blooms, with their large, gray-green deeply-cut leaves and often silvery stems. Grow in full sun on any well-drained soil. For the richest blue flowers grow E. ritro ruthenicus (zones 3–9), which grows to 36 inches, and the cultivar 'Veitch's Blue', up to 4 feet. E. bannaticus 'Taplow Blue' (zones 5–9), grows to 5 feet without the need for staking and has powder blue heads. E. 'Nivalis' has gray-white flowers, pale stems and gray-green foliage and grows to 4 feet.

EPIMEDIUM (Barrenwort, Bishop's Hat)

With the recent introduction of new species from China, interest in these beautiful foliage plants has really taken off. The delicate nodding flowers seem to float above the foliage in spring or early summer. Most flower in white, yellow, pink or mauve, but there are a few orange-flowered kinds such as E. x warleyense and the cultivar 'Orangekönigin'. The heart-shaped leaves have prominent veins and, with the onset of cold weather, often take on bronze, red or purple tints. The new foliage is also colored, and in the deciduous E. grandiflorum 'Nanum', the pale green leaves are edged with chocolate brown.

Erigeron 'Quakeress'

ERIGERON (Fleabane)

One of the most charming of all self-seeders is the wall daisy, Erigeron karvinskianus. The low hummocks of fine stems and tiny leaves bear a constant succession of small daisy blooms throughout the summer. The flowers open white and gradually darken to pink giving a soft, two-tone appearance. They make excellent plants for the front of the border, spilling out over a pathway. They also colonize cracks in paving. Grow on well-drained soil in sun or light shade. Up to 6 inches.

Fleabanes of the herbaceous border are quite different, having much larger individual flowers, some of which are double, in colors ranging from white, through pinks, purples and lavender-blues to deep cerise. For a long time, the pale lilac-pink 'Quakeress' was the standard, but more vivid cultivars have increased. 'Dignity' has violet-purple flowers and is 24 inches tall, and 'Darkest of All' (syn. 'Dunkelste Aller') has deep purple blooms with yellow centers on 30-inch stems.

Grow in full sun on fertile, well-drained but moisture-retentive soil. Water in dry spells. Deadhead to prolong the flowering season, and provide support. Zones 5–8.

Grow this plant in shade on humus-rich, moisture-retentive, well-drained soil giving shelter from extreme cold. Some do withstand dry shade. Clip old foliage from evergreen plants in early spring before the new leaves emerge. E. grandiflorum and E. x youngianum need acid soil. Mulch plants heavily and divide every three or four years.

For pink blooms, try E. grandiflorum 'Rose Queen' (10 inches). Two good whites are 'White Queen' and E. x youngianum 'Niveum' (both 10 inches). For yellow, try E. x perralchicum with bronze spring foliage (16 inches) and E. x versicolor 'Sulphureum', which is an excellent plant for ground cover (12 inches). Zones 5–9.

ERYNGIUM (Sea Holly)

There are two distinct groups of sea holly. One contains plants from the Americas that form evergreen rosettes of sword-shaped, saw-edged leaves and send up impressive stems topped with thimbles or prickly balls. These include Eryngium agavifolium (zones 6–9) and E. eburneum, (zones 9–10), both 5 feet tall. These plants are highly architectural and

Eryngium planum 'Seven Seas'

add an exotic touch to the garden. They tend to suffer when subjected to cold, wet weather, especially if the drainage is less than perfect.

The European, North African and Asian sea hollies are totally different, forming basal clumps of rounded or lobed leaves and highly ornamental flower heads that appear between July and September. The blooms have an everlasting quality and their skeletal form adds to the winter garden. The branching stems and flowers are colored in metallic shades – silvers, blues and violet purples. Some plants, such as E. planum (zones 5–9), which grows to 3 feet, and E. x tripartitum (zones 5–8), 30 inches tall, produce a network of stems studded with many

Euphorbia griffithii 'Fireglow'

small globular heads each sitting on a ring of spines, creating a haze of rich blue. The most spectacular flowers are found in E. alpinum, E. x zabelii and E. x oliverianum (all zones 5–8), which grow to 24 inches. These have large, thimble-shaped flower heads that are surmounted by a striking ruff of colored bracts. In E. alpinum, the bracts are soft and feathery, making an exquisite lacy collar.

E. bourgatii (zones 5–9) has beautiful silver-marbled foliage that is deeply divided. Miss Willmott's ghost, or E. giganteum (zones 5–8), which grows 36 inches tall, is a stunning plant with a broad ruff of jagged silver bracts. It dies after flowering, but produces a plentiful supply of seedlings.

Grow eryngiums in full sun on a fertile, well-drained soil. Dig in plenty of grit to improve drainage, if necessary. The plants are tolerant of poor, gravely soils and lime.

EUPHORBIA
(Milkweed, Spurge)

Euphorbias are highly architectural and often rather strange-looking, partly because, in many cases, the flowers are bright green. Several are evergreen and the colored bracts remain attractive long after flowering; in E. cyparissias (zones 4–9) they turn orange in summer. Most flower in spring before the bulk of herbaceous border plants.

Euphorbia characias wulfenii (zones 7–10), is a sculptural plant with evergreen, blue-gray foliage and large lime-green flower heads that unfurl in early spring. When the heads eventually look a little jaded, cut the stems out at the base to make way for new shoots. It grows 4 feet high.

The wood spurge, E. amygdaloides robbiae (zones 6–9) grows to 24 inches high, though its searching roots can travel some distance to colonize the ground. The glossy, evergreen leaves are arranged in rosettes along the stem. It is a superlative plant for ground cover in dry shade, but also grows happily in sun.

The trailing stems of E. myrsinites (zones 5–8) have angular leaves in light blue-green that bear rounded, lime green flower heads in spring. This evergreen is perfect for a hot spot. It reaches 3x12 inches.

E. cyparissias and forms (zones 4–9) have many upright stems arising from a somewhat invasive rootstock. These are covered in needle-like leaves giving a soft, feathery appearance and the flowers are produced from late spring. It is 12 inches tall.

The flame red or orange flowers of E. griffithii cultivars such as 'Dixter', 'Fireglow' and 'Fern Cottage' that appear in early summer are a break from the usual greeny-yellow shades. The handsome foliage emerges red and retains an overall reddish cast. Plants color best in full sun though they will tolerate partial shade. They like a rich, well-cultivated moisture-retentive soil. You can even grow them in a bog garden. It is 30 inches tall.

E. amygdaloides 'Purpurea' (zones 6–9), 12 inches tall, has purple foliage and E. dulcis 'Chameleon' (zones 4–9) is so-called because, in contrast to the purple foliage, the long-lasting bracts are tinted pink and red in fall. This plant seeds freely, but rarely becomes a nuisance. It grows to 18 inches tall.

Euphorbia sap is a skin irritant and should be washed off immediately.

FESTUCA
(Blue-leaved Fescue)

Fescues are tussock-forming grasses with fine leaves and slender upright flower spikes in early summer. Festuca glauca, blue fescue (zones 4–8), has blue-gray leaves, but forms with a more pronounced blue cast are 'Blaufuchs' (syn. 'Blue Fox'), 'Blauglut' (syn. 'Blue Glow') and 'Elijah Blue'. All grow to around 8 inches in height and spread although the flower stems reach 12 inches.

F. valesiaca 'Silbersee' (syn. 'Silver Sea'), zones 5–9, is a lovely powder blue and is larger overall.

Plant fecues in full sun and well-drained, humus-rich soil. Maintenance includes combing the tussocks with your fingers in spring or early summer to remove old, dead leaves. Every three years, lift the plants, split them in half, remove the congested central core and replant the two halves back to back. Feed and water well.

FOENICULUM VULGARE 'PURPUREUM'
(Bronze Fennel)

A superb background plant for roses and large-flowered perennials, bronze fennel is a must for the mixed border. The haze of purple-bronze, thread-like leaves works well with amber, peach and apricot tones, as well as purples and pinks. In summer, flat yellow flower "umbels" appear at the tops of the tall stems. The plant's skeletal framework makes a fine addition to the winter garden landscape. However, the herb does self-seed and can be a nuisance on light soils. Grow in full sun on any well-drained soil. It reaches 6 feet in height. Zones 4–9.

Festuca glauca

GAURA LINDHEIMERI

This dainty "filler" is finally getting the recognition it deserves and becoming more widely planted. It is one of the longest-flowering perennials, blooming though summer into fall. Because of its open, willowy habit, it can be used to weave through other plants. The clusters of white, pink-tinged blooms seem to hover among other flowers, the effect perfectly described in the name of one of the cultivars 'Whirling Butterflies'. Grow in full sun on well-drained soil. 4 feet high. Zones 6–9.

GERANIUM (Cranesbill)

The cranesbills are a diverse and versatile group, suited to many different situations. The rounded, dish-shaped blooms are produced in abundance, and are often beautifully marked with darker or paler veins. As well as flowers, cranesbills are noted for their foliage, which often is intricately cut,

usually very long-lived, and sometimes has attractive fall coloring. There are blue-flowered geraniums for foreground planting, including 'Johnson's Blue' (zones 4–8) and G. himalayense (zones 4–7) and its cultivars, 'Irish Blue' and 'Gravetye', all of which bloom in early summer (12x18 inches). G. x magnificum (zones 4–8) is taller, at 24 inches, and often has good fall color. Later in summer, G. wallichianum 'Buxton's Variety' (zones 4–8), at 12 inches, has a profusion of small round blooms with a large white central zone highlighted by dark stamens. It continues to flower well into the fall and has luxuriant foliage.

One of the most striking geraniums for a mixed border is G. psilostemon (zones 5–8). This has vivid magenta blooms made all the more dramatic by the central black "eye". Elegantly-cut leaves make a mound reaching 4x4 feet. At it's best in June and July,

Geranium 'Mrs Kendall Clark'

Geranium x riversleaianum 'Mavis Simpson'

this plant continues to produce blooms into the early fall. For sheer flower power, the semi-evergreen cultivars of G. x oxonianum (zones 4–8) are hard to beat. Salmon-pink cultivar 'Wargrave Pink' (24x36 inches) blooms from summer well into the fall. The silvery-pink 'A.T. Johnson' (12x36 inches) and the deep pink 'Claridge Druce' (24x36 inches) are vigorous forms particularly suited to ground cover. If the plants get too unruly in midsummer, cut them back hard with garden shears.

Other floriferous cranesbills are the pink G. x riversleaianum 'Russel Prichard' (zones 6–8) and 'Mavis Simpson', which send out long trailing shoots covered with grayish-green leaves. Both bloom in the summer, and die back in the fall. Try planting dwarf spring bulbs around them to fill the gap before growth recommences in spring. They grow 9x36 inches.

For a sunny, well-drained spot try the alpine G. cinereum 'Ballerina' (zones 5–9) which flowers from early to late summer. The pretty blooms are purplish-pink with a dark center and veining and the gray-green leaves form a neat carpet. It is 4x12 inches.

Most geraniums will tolerate some shade, but a few thrive in it. The mourning widow (G. phaeum, zones 4–8), which flowers in late spring, has purple-black flowers that look moody and vaguely sinister in the half light. The petals are swept back, giving the flowers a dart-like appearance. The white form 'Album' has a cool beauty that few plants can rival at that time of year. 'Lily Lovell' is another excellent selection with large violet-blue flowers. (24x18 inches). Under a particularly dense canopy, try G. nodosum (zones 4–8). It forms glossy hummocks (18x18 inches), and is covered in small lilac flowers most of the year.

Most cranesbills do best when grown on reasonably fertile, humus-rich and moisture-retentive, well-drained soil.

HAKONECHLOA MACRA 'AUREOLA' (Hakone Grass)

The leaves of this Japanese grass are like soft arching ribbons of yellow streaked with green. They taper elegantly to a finely-pointed tip. During summer the whole plant becomes tinged with red, aging to reddish brown toward the fall. Long-lasting flower sprays sometimes appear in late summer. Hakone grass enjoys humus-rich, moisture-retentive soil. It is 16x24 inches. Zones 5–9.

HELICTOTRICHON SEMPERVIRENS (Blue Oat Grass)

This evergreen grass looks a little like a large blue fescue until the sprays of 5-feet high oat-like flowers appear in the summer. The large tussocks of fine silvery-blue leaves, measuring 24x24 inches, work well singly or in clusters in a well-drained sunny border or gravel garden. Comb through the leaves with fingers or a hand-fork in spring to remove debris. Grow on humus-rich soil. Zones 4–9.

HELLEBORUS (Hellebore)

For winter and early spring flowers, the hellebores are unparalleled. They are superb plants for shade, provided the soil is moisture retentive. Many are evergreen plants, with handsome palmate leaves, and all have waxy-textured, very long-lasting blooms. For the widest range of colors, choose good seedling strains of the easily-grown Lenten rose (H. orientalis, zones 4–9). Its large, bowl-shaped blooms come in shades of striking maroon-black through purples, reds and pinks to white, green and pale yellow. Nearly all the forms have beautiful dark speckling around the prominent central boss of stamens. The foliage is deep glossy green and forms a dense mound over which the nodding flowers appear in early

Helleborus foetidus

Hemerocallis 'Mrs David Hall'

The 'Wester Flisk' group has coral red stems and flower stalks. Helleborus foetidus seeds freely. Transplant the seedlings to where they are required as soon as possible. All hellebores resent disturbance after planting.

Grow hellebores in partial or full shade (H. foetidus tolerates full sun and heavy clay) on fertile, humus-rich soil that is well-drained but does not dry out in summer. A late winter mulching on light soils with well-rotted organic matter is beneficial.

HEMEROCALLIS (Daylily)

These trouble-free perennials come in a very wide range of sizes from small-flowered miniatures, less than 12 inches high, to tall cultivars up to 4 feet in height with large, lily-like blooms. You can now get daylilies in an amazing variety of shades from white through yellows, oranges, reds, purples and pinks. Some flowers have a darker or paler zoning in the throat, and others alternate dark and light petals.

The flowers open from clusters of buds formed at the top of leafless, branching stems. Each lasts only a day so it's a good idea to remove faded blooms routinely to make way for the next batch. Most of the cultivars bloom for several weeks between June and August and some, such as the dainty little yellow 'Stella de Oro', are repeat flowering. The narrow, strap-like leaves emerge bright green in spring making an excellent foil for spring flowers such as bulbs. Daylilies are deciduous or evergreen and form steadily-spreading, weed-proof clumps that sometimes color bright yellow in the fall. The evergreen cultivars are less hardy than deciduous types.

spring. They grow to 18x18 inches. It's a good idea to clear away any dead or damaged leaves in late winter before the buds open.

The Christmas rose (H. niger, zones 4–8) is trickier to grow than the Lenten rose, so if you want a white-flowered hellebore, go for one of the white-flowered strains of H. orientalis.

The flowers of H. argutifolius (zones 6–9), appear in clusters at the ends of stout stems in midwinter. They are bright apple green and stand out clearly against the deep grayish-green leaves. The saw-edged foliage is evergreen and of great value throughout the year. It is 36x24 inches.

The stinking hellebore, H. foetidus (zones 6–9), has attractive foliage with narrow tapering "fingers" in very dark green with a glossy sheen. Its flowers are like those of H. argutifolius, and form eye-catching clusters on top of the stems. It is30x24 inches.

Dainty, yellow-flowered species such as Hemerocallis lilioasphodelus (syn. H. flava) come into bloom in late spring and early summer and most of these are deliciously fragrant. You'll also find that many of the yellow and cream-flowered cultivars such as 'Marion Vaughn' and 'Fragrant Treasure' and some red (such as 'Pardon Me') are also beautifully scented.

Daylilies are easy to grow provided they have moist soil (mulch if yours is on the dry side) and full sun. Some of the red and purple ones do better in light shade which prevents scorching. Lift and divide established clumps every three or four years when flowering performance begins to fall off. Zones 3–10.

HESPERIS MATRONALIS
(Dame's Violet)
This is a very old cottage garden plant with simple four-petalled blooms held in loose clusters at the top of straight branching stems in early summer. It is fragrant, especially in the evenings. The seedlings vary in color from white through pastel pinks and mauves to deep lilac purple. Grow in sun or shade on any reasonable soil. After a couple of years the plants become woody and less productive and should be discarded, but they seed freely and there are always new plants to take over. It grows 3 foot high. Zones 4–9.

HEUCHERA
(Coral Bells, Alum Root)
Coral bells are dainty, early summer-flowering perennials with wiry stems supporting clouds of tiny pink, red and sometimes green, cream, or yellow blooms. The rounded evergreen leaves

are often attractively colored and marbled and make a neat basal clump. The Bressingham Hybrids (H. micrantha, zones 4–8) have flowers in cream, pink or red (18x12 inches) and H. 'Red Spangles' (zones 3–8) is taller at 24 inches, with scarlet bells. It often flowers again in late summer. Heuchera cyclindrica 'Greenfinch' and H. 'Green Ivory' (both zones 4–8) have greenish flowers.

The dark, coppery purple-leaved H. micrantha diversifolia 'Palace Purple' (zones 4–8) is grown for its deep purple foliage (24x12 inches). 'Rachel' has similar, excellent foliage and flowers of light coral pink throughout summer into the fall. The dead stems are best removed so as not to detract from the new blooms. H. 'Pewter Moon' is grown for its small, rounded leaves that are rich purple overlaid with silver and

prominent veining. 'Chocolate Ruffles' has glossy, deep purple, frilly-edged leaves and 'Plum Puddin' is another good purple-leaved cultivar.

Grow on moisture-retentive ground in full sun or part shade and mulch to retain moisture. Divide and replant deeply every two or three years and replenish the ground with fertilizer and organic matter.

X HEUCHERELLA ALBA 'BRIDGET BLOOM'
This hybrid of Tiarella and Heuchera flowers in early summer, and then on and off until the fall, producing sprays of light pink blooms over clumps of lobed, light, evergreen leaves. The foliage becomes bronze-tinted in fall. It thrives on moisture-retentive soil and does well in shade. It reaches 16 inches in height. Zones 5–8.

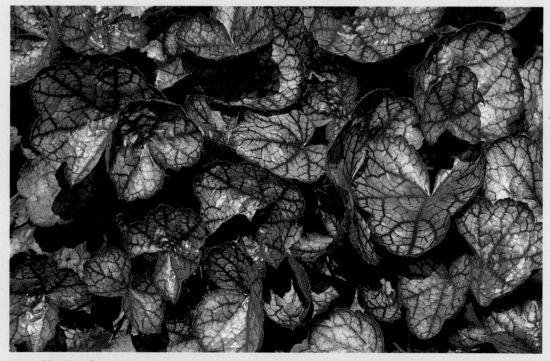

Heuchera 'Pewter Moon'

HOSTA (Plantain Lily)

These are top-class perennials with many attractive features. Their leaves are architectural, many are beautifully variegated, while others may be gold or blue-tinged. Size ranges from giant-leaved specimens such as 'Sum and Substance' (30 inches), to much smaller ground cover types. Even the shape and texture of the leaves varies from broad, heart-shaped blades to narrow and lance shaped (such as Hosta lancifolia), twisted and undulating (such as the white-variegated H. undulata) and smooth, ribbed or puckered (H. sieboldiana 'Elegans'). Variegated cultivars, in particular, look striking as the new foliage unfurls in spring, and in the fall many become a translucent, buttery yellow.

Although chiefly grown for their foliage, some are noted for their elegant blooms in white or purple which appear on upright stems. Several are fragrant, like the white-flowered H. 'Royal Standard'.

Contrary to popular belief, many hostas will grow in full sun provided the soil is moisture retentive, and they will take quite dry conditions if they are grown in shade. Hostas delight in moisture, however, and make superb bog garden plants. Large-leaved hostas create a subtropical atmosphere, and when they are grown with ferns, grasses and bamboos, they take on a distinctly oriental look to them.

The chief problem is protecting buds and fresh new leaves from slug and snail damage. Deer also love to feast on hostas. Hostas make good specimen plants for large pots on the patio and tend to suffer less damage grown this way. Zones 3–8.

Hosta undulata

HOLCUS MOLLIS 'ALBOVARIEGATUS' (Velvet Grass)

This is a bright white-variegated grass that forms a carpet of softly-hairy tufted foliage as it creeps steadily underground. Unlike some spreading grasses, it is not unduly invasive. It is ideal for the front of a shady border. The foliage is brightest in spring and fall when it gets a second flush of growth. Between June and August, very pale green flower panicles grow to 12 inches. Grow in moisture-retentive soil in sun or shade. The plant reaches 6x18 inches. Zones 5–9.

HOUTTUYNIA CORDATA 'CHAMELEON'

This brightly-colored invasive perennial thrives in moist soil, though it tolerates all but very dry conditions. Given a moderate amount of sun, the carpet of heart-shaped leaves that emerges in late spring is variegated red, yellow, green and amber. It has small white flowers in summer. Use as ground cover in the bog garden, to give summer and fall color in a bare patch of ground, or to fill containers on the patio. It grows to 4 inches tall, with an indefinite spread. Zones 6–11.

INULA

These daisy-flowered perennials have an Oriental feel because of the architectural foliage and large yellow blooms. The giant of the group is Inula magnifica (zones 5–8). It produces a great mound of large, coarse, lance-shaped leaves and flowers on 6-foot stems in late summer with a spread of around 3 feet. Grow in a sheltered spot to prevent wind damage. The ancient medicinal herb, elecapane (I. helenium, zones 5–8) is fairly similar but doesn't have quite the same dramatic effect.

Inula hookeri (zones 4–8) has greenish-yellow blooms which also appear in late summer. Despite its somewhat invasive tendencies, it is well worth growing, especially on its own in damp soil or with other robust foliage perennials in a bog garden. It reaches 30x24 inches.

Inula ensifolia (zones 4–9) is the one most suited to a mixed border, growing to 18x12 inches, with narrow foliage. It produces its daisy flowers in midsummer with wide, short petals.

IRIS

In recent years, the early summer-flowering tall bearded irises have grown in popularity due to their architectural form (a prerequisite for many modern gardens) and drought tolerance. They produce fans of gray-green sword-shaped leaves and sturdy stems bearing several large sculpted blooms with upright petals called "standards" and drooping petals called "falls." Almost every color is represented. Some are bicolored, while others are beautifully marked or suffused with other shades. A few are fragrant.

Height is normally around 3 feet but there are taller and shorter ones. Iris pallida (zones 5–9) is similar in appearance to the bearded irises and the cultivar 'Variegata' has striking foliage with leaves boldly striped yellow and gray-green. It produces soft lavender-blue flowers.

For moist border soil, there are the dainty Iris sibirica cultivars (zones 4–9), mainly in shades of blue and purple but also with white, pink and yellow forms. These make clumps of grassy foliage and slender, strongly upright stems bearing many small

Inula hookeri

Bearded Irises, among them 'Patterdale'

KNAUTIA MACEDONICA

One of the most long-flowered of all perennials, it produces a profusion of small, crimson-red pincushion flowers in mid- and late summer. The wiry, lightly-branched stems curve up from the base and the plant tends to loll into other plants, interweaving with their flowers. It is particularly good planted among silver-leaved plants and pastel-colored flowers. The leaves are small and insignificant. Grow in full sun on any well-drained soil, especially one rich in lime. It reaches 24x18 inches. Zones 5–9.

KNIPHOFIA
(Red Hot Poker, Tritoma)

Only some of these plants have the poker-like flowers which graduate from yellow through orange to red that gave this genus its common name. One of the best of this type is the 3–4 foot tall 'Royal Standard' (zones 6–9) that flowers in late summer. The narrow, strap-like foliage is evergreen to semi-evergreen and forms a mound from which the single flower stems rise.

There is no problem with color scheming since there are single-color species as well as cultivars that flower in green, cream, yellow, orange or flame-red shades between midsummer and the fall. One of the best recently-introduced dwarf kniphofias is the dainty cream 'Little Maid' (24x18 inches) which forms clumps of fine, grassy foliage.

Grow kniphofias on free-draining soil that is not too rich or overfed. Keep the plants well-watered during the summer months. Mulch crowns as protection from cold in winter.

blooms in early summer. They also have attractive seed pods and reach 24–36 inches. For the bog garden or stream side, choose the showy Japanese water iris, Iris ensata (syn. I. kaempferi) cultivars (zones 5–8) which flower from early to midsummer and reach 24–36 inches.

The purple-black Iris chrysographes (zones 7–9) also thrives in moisture, but will grow in a damp border that has been heavily mulched. It is similar in form to I. sibirica and flowers between late spring and early summer, growing up to 16 inches.

Some irises are tolerant of shade and quite dry soil conditions. One of the toughest is the gladdon iris (Iris foetidissima, zones 7–9), which has handsome strap-shaped evergreen leaves, insignificant mauve flowers, and large pods splitting to reveal brilliant orange berries in fall. The plant reaches 20 inches. It makes excellent ground cover for dry shade under trees. The green and white striped 'Variegata' is one of the most striking evergreen perennials.

The late spring-flowering Pacific Coast hybrids, or Californian Group, contains plants which work well in the shade of trees provided the soil is neutral to acid, humus rich and moisture retentive. The flowers open out flat and come in a range of subtle shades. The plants grow 6–24 inches tall.

LAMIUM
(Deadnettle)

The deadnettles carpet the ground with heart-shaped, semi-evergreen leaves. In early summer, whorls of hooded flowers appear. Forms of Lamium maculatum have silvery-white variegated foliage and thrive in shade. 'White Nancy' is one of the best cultivars, with bright silver foliage and white flowers. 'Beacon Silver' has the same silver leaf, usually mottled with purple spots, and the flowers are a vivid purple-pink. 'Pink Pewter' is a pink-flowered variant with an overall green cast to the silver while 'Roseum' has green leaves with a central white stripe, and blooms in a pretty pale pink. 'Chequers' is similar to 'Roseum', but with purple blooms. Good yellow-leaved forms include 'Aureum' and 'Cannon's Gold', both of which have contrasting purple flowers and thrive in light shade.

In spring, before growth starts again, tidy up the plants by cutting the shoots back to ground level. You'll see the mat of new leaves beginning to emerge at the base. Do this again after each main flush of bloom to encourage a fresh crop of younger, brighter leaves, and you'll often be rewarded by more flowers as well. On fertile, moisture-retentive soil the plants can be very productive. Mulch plants on drier soils, particularly those grown in full sun, as dry conditions promote mildew in these plants. They reach 8–16x36 inches.

Another group of ground-covering deadnettles are derived from Lamium galeobdolon, otherwise known as the yellow archangel. 'Florentinum' (syn. 'Variegatum') is a rampant ground cover

Kniphofia 'Alcazar'

Liatris spicata 'Kobold'

plant for the wild garden with yellow blooms in summer and silver zoning on the green leaves. The height is about 12 inches and the spread indefinite. The cultivar 'Hermann's Pride' is much less invasive than the species and has a very striking pattern of silver netting on its handsome leaves. Zones 4–8.

LEUCANTHEMUM X SUPERBUM (Shasta Daisy)

The common shasta daisy has simple white daisy-like flowers with yellow centers on tall stems from early summer through late fall. It looks at home in most styles of garden and reaches 36x24 inches.

For shorter-growing cultivars, try 'Silberprinzesschen' (syn. 'Little Princess') at 18 inches tall or the pure white 'Snow Lady' at only 10 inches. Both 'Bishopstone' and 'Phyllis Smith' have enchanting fringed petals and are about 30 inches in height. 'Aglaia', at 36 inches tall, and the shorter-growing 'Esther Read' both have attractive semi-double blooms.

'Wirral Supreme' and 'T.E. Killin' are anemone-centered with a host of little petals replacing the yellow "eye" (both 36 inches high).

Grow in full sun or light shade on any reasonably fertile soil, especially alkaline, moisture-retentive types. Divide and replant every couple of years. Zones 5–8.

LIATRIS SPICATA (Gayfeather, Blazing Star)

With its tufts of grass-like foliage and stiff, bottlebrush flowers of a rich mauve-pink, the gayfeather looks very much at home in a modern setting.

The blooms of 'Kobold' (syn. 'Goblin') and 'Floristan Violett' are even more vivid, and if you want white flowers, try the white variety 'Alba' or 'Floristan Weiss'. All cultivars flower in late summer and early fall. Grow in full sun on moisture-retentive, well-drained soil. Deadhead gayfeather to prolong its flowering period. These plants reach 18x12 inches. Zones 4–9.

LIBERTIA PEREGRINANS

One of a growing number of New Zealand plants that have made their way into gardens in recent years, this libertia will appeal to those with an eye for the unusual. The stiff fans of evergreen grass-like leaves have a broad central band of orange and this gives the whole plant an orange glow. Sprays of small white flowers are produced in early to midsummer and are followed by interesting yellow or orange seed capsules. The plant throws up new leaf fans some way from the original crown, producing attractive combinations, especially when planted with low ground cover plants. Grow libertia in light, well-drained soil in full sun or part shade and insulate the roots in winter in cold regions. It reaches 18x36 inches. Zones 8–10.

LIGULARIA

These moisture-loving perennials have architectural foliage and bold-colored flowers. In Ligularia dentata 'Desdemona' and the similar 'Othello', the large, rounded to heart-shaped leaves are a dark, brownish green above, with a reverse of deep mahogany. From summer to early fall, vivid orange daisies appear. The plant

grows to 4 feet tall, with a spread of 24 inches. The cultivar 'Gregynog Gold' is taller at 6 feet and produces an impressive cone-shaped spike of orange daisies over a mound of huge, rounded leaves.

Ligularia przewalskii has dark, deeply-cut leaves and almost black stems carrying tall, tapering yellow flower spires on a plant of 5 feet tall, with a spread of 36 inches. 'The Rocket' is another excellent form with lemon yellow flowers in July. It grows to about 6 feet in height.

Grow these handsome plants in rich, moist soil in full sun or partial shade. On drier soils, shade is essential to prevent the plants from wilting. Provide shelter from strong winds which can damage the large leaves. Zones 4–8.

LIRIOPE MUSCARI (Lilyturf)

The flowers of this fall-blooming perennial look a little like those of the grape hyacinth (Muscari), with its spikes of tiny, rounded blooms. The glossy leaves are evergreen and form dense, grassy tufts from which the mauve flower spikes appear in early fall. Look out for improved forms such as L. muscari 'Big Blue' and 'Majestic' which have rich violet-purple flowers. For white flowers choose the elegant cultivar 'Monro White'.

Grow in full sun on a well-drained soil containing a plentiful supply of humus. Liriope will tolerate some shade, but it won't flower as freely as it does in a sunny site. Remove dead leaves and flower spikes regularly to keep plants neat. The mounds will reach 12x18 inches. Zones 6–10.

LYCHNIS CORONARIA
(Dusty Miller)

Dusty miller seeds round the garden, preferring sunny well-drained spots and gravel. The young plants are easily recognized, forming rosettes of gray felted leaves. They are easy to move around. In midsummer, branching flower stems bear many rounded vivid cerise-pink blooms. The stems become silvery toward the tips and this helps to emphasize the color of the flowers. The white-flowered 'Alba' has even more pronounced silver coloring and makes a focal point in a border.

With their airy habit, both pink and white lychnis make good "minglers" for the mixed border, and are useful for breaking up the line of low front-of-the-border plantings. They grow to 24x18 inches. Zones 4–8.

LYSIMACHIA
NUMMULARIA
(Creeping Jenny)

A great plant for low, semi-evergreen ground cover in the bog garden or any moisture-retentive soil in shade. It sends out long streamers of rounded leaves, and roots where it touches the ground. Lysimachia nummularia 'Aurea' has stunning, yellow-green foliage. In early summer, lemon-yellow buttercup-like flowers are produced in the leaf axils. It is a diminuitive 2 inches tall, but spreads to around 36 inches. Zones 4–8.

MACLEAYA (Plume Poppy)

The leaves of this tall perennial are quite exceptional. Reminiscent of grape vine leaves, they are beautifully sculpted. An ideal backdrop for a mixed border, Macleaya microcarpa produces a mass of upright stems covered in gray-green foliage that is almost white beneath. Despite its stature, it only needs staking in exposed gardens. The mid- to late summer flower plumes are white in the species and deep coral pink in the improved cultivar 'Kelway's Coral Plume'. Care should be taken as this plant is moderately invasive, so don't plant near timid neighbors.

M. cordata is very similar, but with larger flower plumes. Look out for 'Flamingo' with buff-pink plumes. Grow in full sun or light shade on deeply cultivated, moist but well-drained soil. Mulch heavily to conserve moisture in drier conditions. It reaches 6 feet in height. Zones 4–9.

MALVA MOSCHATA ALBA
(White Musk Mallow)

The white form of the common musk mallow is an elegant plant that will combine easily with many other types of flowers, blooming over a long period from early summer onward. The leaves are deeply cut and make an excellent foil for the clusters of satin-textured, cup-shaped blooms. This

Lychnis coronaria

plant, fortunately, seeds itself readily in the border so there is always a fresh supply of plants to take over when others are discarded. Grow in full sun on well-drained soil. Tolerates poor, stony soil. It grows to 24x18 inches. Zones 4–8.

MATTEUCCIA STRUTHIOPTERIS (Ostrich fern)

All ferns are architectural, but this individual has a striking form. The rich green fronds are especially bright in spring and form tall, upright "shuttle-cocks" that spread via rhizomes to form little colonies. This plant tends to be past its best by August. Remove dead fronds to keep it tidy. It grows well in damp woodland, shady bog gardens, or next to water. It reaches 36 inches tall with a spread of 24 inches. Zones 3–8.

MECONOPSIS CAMBRICA (Welsh Poppy)

Unlike the blue Himalayan poppies and their relatives, the Welsh poppy is an easily-grown plant. The citrus yellow or rich orange blooms look as though they're made of tissue paper, making the plant look distinctly oriental. Flowering begins in late spring when they combine really well with bluebells (Hyacithoides), but they bloom on and off for several months. Pompon-headed doubles in either color are also available. 'Francis Perry' is a rarely-seen red form. Grow Welsh poppies on moisture-retentive ground in partial to deep shade. Transplant seedlings as early as possible to avoid damaging the developing tap root. They grow to 12x12 inches. Zones 6–8.

Matteuccia struthiopteris

MENTHA (Mint)

All members of the mint family have a deserved reputation as being rampant colonizers and spreaders and it is usually suggested that they are planted in bottomless buckets, sunk in the border, to curb their spread. They are still, however, liable to escape but there are some that are worth growing anyway because they are such

Miscanthus sinensis 'Variegatus'

MILIUM EFFUSUM 'AUREUM' (Bowles' Golden Grass, Golden Wood Millet)

This is an ideal partner for blue, white or orange spring flowers because of its bright acid-yellow foliage which fades to butter yellow with age. The plants develop loose tufts of soft arching leaves and in early summer, bear 24-inch tall dainty flower spikes. It self-sows, but is never a nuisance. Grow in partial shade on humus-rich, moisture-retentive soil. Dry conditions promote mildew. Up to 12x18 inches. Zones 6–9.

MISCANTHUS SINENSIS (Eulalia Grass)

Miscanthus is a tall ornamental grass grown for its strong architectural contribution to the garden. Most hybrids develop good fall coloring, and the red or purple-brown flower heads that appear in fall fade to a biscuit or silver color in winter and remain highly ornamental through until spring. Plants may not flower, however, in areas that are very cold.

The striped Miscanthus sinensis 'Variegatus' makes a fountain of bright foliage variegated with white stripes running longitudinally along the length of the leaves. It reaches 6 feet in height. In contrast, zebra grass (M. sinensis 'Zebrinus') has yellow horizontal banding all the way up the leaf. In shade, or when back lit, this plant gives the effect of dappled sun. It reaches 7 feet in height.

The porcupine grass, M. sinensis 'Strictus' is also attractively striped and the plant has a stiff, dense habit. The narrow columns of maiden grass, 'Gracillimus', that arch out at the tips,

decorative plants. Two varieties in particular have beautifully-variegated foliage and can be left to intermingle with other plants provided the others are all reasonably robust. The first is the variegated apple mint (Mentha suaveolens 'Variegata', zones 6–9) with its sweet-smelling leaves that are heavily variegated with rich creamy white. Ginger mint (M. x gracilis 'Variegata', zones 6–9) has prominent yellow veining. Grow in sun or shade on moisture-retentive soil and cut stems hard back in summer to promote fresh new growth. They grow to 16 inches tall and spread indefinitely.

MERTENSIA PULMONARIOIDES (Virginia Bluebells)

Like so many of its relatives in the borage family, Virginia bluebells brings the color blue to the garden. The smooth oval blue-green leaves make a lovely foil for the drooping clusters of violet blue bell-shaped flowers in the spring. Unfortunately, the plant dies away soon after flowering, leaving a gap by midsummer. Fill the hole with seasonal bedding plants. Grow in shade on cool, humus-rich or peaty, moisture-retentive ground. It grows to 18x12 inches. Zones 3–7.

are composed of very narrow blades and make a valuable foliage contrast for broad-leaved subjects planted close by. Curling flower tassels are produced in the fall. The height is 4 feet. The foliage of 'Morning Light' is distinguished by its white leaf margins that give the plant a pretty, silvery effect. This light, airy plant grows up to 36 inches high.

For a more free-flowering cultivar, choose 'Silberfeder' (syn. 'Silver Feather') with feathery silvery-pink heads held well above the ribbon-like leaves that bloom in early to midfall, remaining throughout the winter months. It reaches 8 feet in height. For smaller gardens, choose compact forms such as 'Kleine Silberspinne' (syn. 'Little Silver Spider') as well as 'Kleine Fontäne' (syn. 'Little Fountain'), and 'Yakushima Dwarf'. All grow to form clumps 36x36 inches.

Miscanthus will grow happily in average-quality soil that is not too dry. They will tolerate both sun or partial shade. Zones 4–9.

MOLINIA CAERULEA 'ARUNDINACEA VARIEGATA'

This dainty, cream-variegated grass is perfect for the front of a border or for forming a neat edge to a border. The arching leaves, sometimes pink-tinged, form tufts that spread slowly. In early fall, cream stalks appear bearing the airy purple panicles of flowers. Even when faded to parchment, this grass remains attractive well into the fall. Plant in moisture-retentive, humus-rich, acidic soil in sun or part shade. It reaches 24x12 inches. Zones 5–9.

MONARDA (Bee Balm, Bergamot, Oswego Tea)

Bee balm has a very pleasing form with upright stems clothed in pointed aromatic leaves and hooded flowers with contrasting bracts from June to September. As its name suggests, it is a magnet for bees and butterflies. For many years 'Croftway Pink' (zones 4–8), 'Cambridge Scarlet' (zones 4–9), and purplish-pink 'Beauty of Cobham' (zones 4–9), reigned supreme. But in recent years, plant breeders have crossed the moisture-loving Monarda didyma with the more drought-tolerant M. fistulosa, creating a range of new hybrids and some dramatic new colors. Look out for cultivars named after signs of the zodiac such as 'Capricorn' with purple green foliage and pink flowers (zones 4–9), and ones named after North American Indian tribes. Purple-toned hybrids tend to be more tolerant of dry soils. Plants grown in moist soil can spread rapidly. They grow to 3–4 feet in height, with an 18-inch spread. Grow on moisture-retentive ground with a high organic

Monarda 'Beauty of Cobham'

127

Nepeta nervosa

content and mulch plants annually, especially on drier soils. Deadhead when the flowers fade. Divide and replant every three years. Good rich-colored cultivars include 'Mahogany' (dark wine-red, zones 4–9), 'Squaw' (vermilion, zones 4–9), 'Scorpion' and 'Prärienacht' syn. 'Prairie Night' (dark lilac pink, zones 4–8).

NECTAROSCORDUM SICULUM BULGARICUM

At first sight, this bulb looks like one of the large-flowered alliums. In late spring, it has the most elegant blooms – around 30 little hanging bells on fine arching filaments coming out of the top of a single 3-foot stem. The flower color is a creamy green, flushed with mauve. Eventually the flowers turn upward and the seed pods group together, giving the appearance of a fairy-tale castle in Bavaria. Plant the bulbs in fall in groups between lower-growing plants, spacing them 10–16 inches apart. Grow in fertile, well-drained soil in full sun or part shade. Zones 6–10.

NEPETA (Catmint)

The common catmint (Nepeta x faassenii, zones 4–8) is one of the most valuable of all summer-flowering perennials making a superb filigree "filler" for the front of a border, with a froth of soft lavender-purple blooms that almost obscure the small gray green leaves. At its best in June, it continues to flower into the fall, especially when sheared over after the first flush. It grows to 18x18 inches, but the slightly darker 'Six Hills Giant' (zones 4–8) grows to double that and is hardier in cold areas. The pure white catmint, N. racemosa 'Snowflake' (zones 4–8) is neat and compact at only 12 inches tall and flowers from early to midsummer.

A catmint with large, individual blooms of Spode blue, held in loose spikes, is the vigorous Nepeta sibirica 'Souvenir d'André Chaudron' (syn. 'Blue Beauty', zones 5–9). It flowers from early summer onward and measures 20x24 inches. N. nervosa (zones 5–9) makes a mound of green foliage topped by short, thick flower spikes of light blue. It flowers mid-summer to the fall and measures 14x24 inches.

OENOTHERA (Evening Primrose)

There are some excellent low-growing evening primroses that flower over a long period and work particularly well in a gravel garden or within a paved area. Oenothera macrocarpa (syn. O. missouriensis, zones 5–8), commonly known as Ozark's sundrops, has large golden yellow blooms from late spring to the fall, and spreading stems carrying narrow pointed leaves. It grows to 6x8 inches. The fragrant

Nepeta x faassenii

rich yellow blooms of Oenothera fruticosa 'Fyrverkeri' (syn. 'Fireworks', zones 4–8), grace the garden from mid- to late summer. The plant's stems and flower buds are red, making an attractive contrast to the yellow blossoms. It reaches 16 inches in height. Cultivars of the fragrant white evening primrose, Oenothera speciosa (zones 5–8), have large blooms from early summer right through to the fall. Pink-flowered cultivars include the pretty 'Pink Petticoats', 'Rosea' and 'Siskiyou'. All reach 12x18 inches and thrive on free-draining soil in full sun.

ONOCLEA SENSIBILIS
(Sensitive Fern)
This moisture-loving fern, suitable for a bog garden, has arching, triangular green fronds that in spring unfurl upright and are colored pinky-bronze. These sterile fronds die away after the first frost, but the fertile, spore-producing fronds, which are dark brown, remain through winter. It measures 24x24 inches. Zones 4–9.

OPHIOPOGON PLANISCAPUS 'NIGRESCENS'
Near-black foliage characterizes this tough ground-covering perennial that grows in arching clumps of narrow leaves. It spreads via runners, and in time makes a dense carpet suitable for full sun or moderate shade where it keeps its coloring remarkably well. Ophiopogon is drought tolerant and should be grown on well-drained soil. In late summer, insignificant purple-tinged blooms are followed by black berries. It reaches 10x12 inches. Zones 6–10.

ORIGANUM
(Ornamental Marjoram)
The common marjoram, Origanum vulgare (zones 5–9) thrives in hot dry places, colonizing the edges of sunny borders and self-seeding inoffensively in gravel gardens. The aromatic leaves are small and are obscured from mid-summer to fall by wiry upright stems carrying tiny soft lilac blooms with darker bracts. It reaches 12 inches tall, with a spread of 36 inches.

Golden marjoram (O. vulgare 'Aureum') forms a low carpet of rounded bright golden leaves in spring which gradually darken to lime green as the season progresses. Its flowers are insignificant and plants actually look neater if the flower stems are removed as they appear.

O. laevigatum 'Herrenhausen' (zones 7–10) has purple-tinged leaves in winter and large flower clusters in summer. It grows to 24 inches tall.

Origanum vulgare

Penstemon 'Ruby'

OSMUNDA REGALIS
(Royal Fern)

This is one of the largest of the hardy ferns with fronds reaching 5 feet in ideal conditions. It needs moist soil and can be grown in a moist, shady border that has been heavily mulched or in a bog garden. Royal ferns look stunning next to water and work well planted singly so that their statuesque form can be fully appreciated. The sterile fronds that unfurl from their woody base in spring are at first copper tinted. The narrow upright fertile fronds produced in summer are rusty brown, making a fine contrast with the green foliage. Even in fall the plant has something to offer as its leaves turn to a rich yellow. Clumps reach 5x3 feet. Zones 4–9.

OSTEOSPERMUM JUCUNDUM

Tender osteospermums have become popular for summer containers, but there is a small number of evergreen, woody osteospermums that survive mild winters unscathed, particularly in full sun where the ground is sharply-drained. Osteospermum jucundum is one of the hardiest, producing a long succession of soft mauve daisy-like flowers that have a dark "eye" and darker reverse to the petals. Its spoon-shaped leaves form dense mats; the plants are particularly effective cascading over the top of a low wall or out onto a patio or paving. They bloom throughout summer into the fall. O. j. compactum has pinker flowers and those of 'Lady Leitrim' are white with a mauve reverse, on slightly taller stems. Plants form mounds up to 8x24 inches. Zones 9–10.

Osmunda regalis

PAEONIA (Peony)

Flowering late spring to early summer, these long-lived perennials add luxury with their flamboyant blooms. Most popular are cultivars of P. lactiflora, but several hardier species have also come to the fore. Single blooms showing the boss of yellow stamens, as well as fragrant cultivars, are in demand. Singles are more weather-resistant than doubles but double blooms last longer and are more freely produced. Colors range from white and yellow through pinks and reds. The handsome, deeply-cut leaves often develop good fall tints and spring shoots are sometimes dark purple or red. Grow in sun on fertile, well-drained soil, and leave undisturbed. 24 inches tall.

PENSTEMON (Beard Tongue)

The spires of flared tubular flowers come in a wide range of shades from white through pinks, reds and purples. Some have many small, narrow blooms while others have fewer, larger and often more showy flowers with contrasting throat colors. In recent years, gardeners have begun to realize that these superlative late bloomers are hardy given the right growing conditions. Cultivars with small narrow leaves are more cold tolerant than those with large, broad leaves, but all need a free-draining soil as winter drainage is a critical factor. Plants benefit from spring planting so that they have the whole season to establish before winter. Trim away woody stems at the start of the season, cutting just above new shoots. Deadhead to encourage more flowers and stake tall, large-flowered cultivars in exposed sites.

There are low-growing cultivars at 12–18 inches tall, including the hardy, pink-flowered 'Evelyn' (zones 7–10), as well as plants growing up to 36 inches. Some of the best include 'Pink Endurance' (zones 6–9), 'Alice Hindley' (soft mauve and white, zones 7–10), 'Apple Blossom' (pale pink and white, zones 4–9), 'Osprey' (white with pink edges), 'Blackbird' (deep burgundy), 'Ruby' (rich red), all zones 7–10, 'Stapleford Gem' (purple, blue and green, zones 6–9), and 'Rubicundus' (large scarlet red with white throats).

PEROVSKIA (Russian Sage)

In midsummer, stiff, upright white stems carry airy sprays of tiny violet-blue flowers on this subshrub. The display continues into fall and in winter, the stems are a ghostly white and look beautiful when frosted. The deeply-cut, gray-green leaves are aromatic. 'Blue Spire' is a very good form. Grow in full sun on any well-drained soil and cut the stems back to ground level in early spring. It forms upright clumps up to 4 feet tall. Zones 6–9.

PERSICARIA (Knotweed)

One of the best plants of this genus for general border planting is P. amplexicaulis 'Firetail' (zones 5–8). This is a tall, self-supporting plant that produces a mound of large pointed leaves and many slender stems topped with narrow, crimson-red flower spikes. The display lasts from midsummer until the frosts. It reaches 4x4 feet, or more with moisture. Grow on moisture-retentive ground in full sun or light shade. The pink-flowered bistort (P. bistorta 'Superba', zones 4–8), likes moist soil, so grow at the water's edge, in a bog garden or moist, lightly-shaded border. It flowers in early summer, forming fluffy poker-like heads, and continues for many weeks. It sometimes flowers again later on. It measures 30x24 inches.

PHLOMIS RUSSELIANA (Sticky Jerusalem Sage)

Looking rather like the shrubby Jerusalem sage (Phlomis fruticosa), this evergreen perennial has rather coarse, heart-shaped foliage that is felted and gray-green in color. Despite its height of 36 inches, this woody plant makes excellent ground cover. Upright stems bear whorls of hooded, butter-yellow blooms in summer. The sturdy stems should be left on the plant for winter decoration and cut to the base in spring. Grow in full sun on well-drained soil. Zones 4–9.

PHUOPSIS STYLOSA

This aromatic, front-of-the-border plant is perfect for softening the edges, especially where it is allowed to creep out over paving. The pretty narrow, light green leaves are set in whorls and make a carpet above which the rounded clusters of tiny pink blooms appear through summer. Suitable for a sunny, well-drained spot. It reaches 6x20 inches. Zones 5–8.

Perovskia 'Blue Spire'

Pleioblastus auricomus

PLATYCODON GRANDIFLORUS
(Balloon Flower)

Flowering from midsummer to the fall, this very old garden plant, originally from the Far East, is appreciated for its large balloon-shaped flower buds that open wide to display five broad petals. The flowers of the species are deep mauve-blue and the simple, lance-shaped leaves also have a bluish tint. It grows to 24x12 inches. There are several excellent varieties including whites and doubles. 'Mariesii' is shorter at only 16 inches, and earlier flowering with deep-blue blooms. Plant in average-quality, well-drained soil in sun or part shade. Zones 4–9.

PLEIOBLASTUS AURICOMUS

In late spring, needle-like shoots emerge from the ground and unfurl to give bright yellow, green-streaked oblong leaves that are sharply pointed.

This slowly-creeping bamboo produces strong, upright, leafy stems. In damp soils, it grows tall and colonizes well, but in an ordinary border situation it is very well behaved. Radiant in fall sunshine, in mild areas it continues to shine for most of the winter. Cut back to ground level before growth begins in spring for larger, better quality leaves. Enjoys humus-rich, moisture-retentive soil in sun or part shade. It reaches 4 feet tall. Zones 7–11.

POLEMONIUM CAERULEUM
(Jacob's Ladder)

This cottage garden perennial has green ladder-like foliage with leaves arranged in pairs. In early summer, many upright stems arise from the basal clump and carry sprays of soft lavender-blue, cup-shaped blooms with prominent orange stamens. It self-seeds, making useful replacements for these short-lived plants. Deadhead to control seeding and to encourage further blooms. The variety 'Alba' has particularly attractive white flowers. Jacob's ladder prefers a moisture-retentive soil and grows in full sun or partial shade. It grows up to 24x24 inches. Zones 4–8.

POLYPODIUM (Polypody)

The wall polypody, Polypodium vulgare (zones 6–8), has narrow, evergreen leathery fronds. New fronds are produced from a spreading rhizome. In humid, moist climates, it can be seen growing on tree branches and in crevices in walls. However, it is tolerant of dry shade, and prefers acid soil. It grows to 16x24 inches. There are many interesting forms of the wall polypody, as well as the very similar P. cambricum (zones 6–8). The fronds of the intermediate polypody (P. interjectum) are broader and it makes an excellent colonizer for a sunny or shady spot, preferably on alkaline soil.

POLYSTICHUM
(Shield Ferns)

The hard shield fern, Polystichum aculeatum (zones 3–6), is an evergreen with leathery, glossy, rich green fronds that are long, narrow, and highly dissected. It measures 20x12 inches. The hedge fern, P. setiferum (zones 6–9), has a larger crown than the hard shield fern, with elegantly cut fronds covered in dense scales. Both enjoy moisture-retentive, slightly acid soil with a high humus content, and shade, though the hedge fern can tolerate some sun and drier conditions than the hard shield fern. The fresh green fronds stand out perfectly against a carpet of fall leaves.

PULMONARIA (Lungwort)

These are low, spring-flowering plants for shade, usually with clusters of soft blue, mauve or pink bell-shaped blooms. Some are grown chiefly for their attractive lance-shaped leaves, which can either be silver spotted, as in the white-flowered Pulmonaria officinalis 'Sissinghurst White' (zones 6–8), to virtually completely silvery-white with a narrow green margin as in P. saccharata Argentea Group (zones 4–8). Those of P. rubra 'David Ward' are green with white margins.

The flowers of P. angustifolia (zones 4–8) are rich blue and those of P. rubra 'Redstart' (zones 5–8) appear very early and are reddish-pink. There are many other excellent cultivars to choose from, generally measuring 12x18–24 inches. Grow in moisture-retentive, humus-rich soil in shade. Cut back hard once the foliage begins to look a little tired in summer, feed and water thoroughly to encourage a fresh crop of leaves to last into fall.

Pulmonaria rubra 'David Ward'

RHEUM PALMATUM 'ATROSANGUINEUM' (Chinese Rhubarb)

In spring in the bog garden, strange and enormous alien-like buds begin to unfurl and huge jaggedly-cut leaves of deep beet red appear. As they expand, they become greener with a red suffusion and dark undersides, a perfect foil for the towering, crimson-red flower spike that appears in early or midsummer above the striking mound of leaves.

The flowers themselves are deep red and tiny, but the overall effect of the flower spike is really rather spectacular. Remove the spike as soon as it begins to fade unless you want to collect seed. Remove also any discolored leaves. If you want extra large leaves, remove the spike when it first appears. Grow in sun or light shade in a permanently moist spot, rich in organic matter such as a pool side or bog garden. It reaches an impressive 8x6 feet. Zones 5–9.

RHODANTHEMUM HOSMARIENSE

This delightful bushy subshrub, with intensely silver, finely-dissected evergreen foliage arising from a woody base, forms a spreading hummock over which curving stems carry a multitude of white daisy blooms. It has an exceptionally long flowering period from spring to fall and benefits from being clipped over with shears in midsummer to maintain a good habit. Grow in full sun on well-drained soil. It is particularly effective planted in a gravel garden, tumbling over a low retaining wall, or grown in containers. It reaches 12x12 inches. Zones 9–10.

RODGERSIA

Architectural foliage, rich fall tints and fluffy flower plumes characterize these moisture-loving perennials. One of the best is Rodgersia pinnata 'Superba' which has large, paired bronzy leaflets and showy pink flower heads in midsummer that grow more than 20 inches long. The plant measures 33x36 inches.

The jagged and triangular leaflets of Rodgersia podophylla are deeply veined and bronze tinted when young, developing dark copper later in the season. Its flowers are creamy white and the plant grows up to 36 inches.

Rodgersia aesculifolia has bronze-tinged crinkled leaves like those of a giant horse chestnut. The flowers are white tinged pink and fragrant. It reaches 4x3 feet. Grow in a position sheltered from wind, in shade or in a moist, sunny spot. They will benefit from heavy spring mulching. These are ideal plants for bog gardens and waterside plantings. Zones 5–8.

ROMNEYA COULTERI
(Californian Tree Poppy)

Huge white tissue-paper blooms with a central boss of golden yellow stamens are the hallmark of the Californian tree poppy. This tall, elegant plant is somewhat shrubby in nature, but is treated as an herbaceous perennial and the stems cut back to the base in late fall. Its leaves are a perfect foil for the flowers: gray and deeply lobed.

Romneya is sensitive to disturbance and competition, but once established in the right conditions, this plant can spread vigorously through a border so take care not to plant it near less aggressive plants that could be swamped by it. 'White Cloud' has lighter gray leaves, fine flowers, and is more vigorous than the species. Grow romneya in full sun on free-draining soil. Protect young plants from spring frosts for the first few years, and in cold regions, grow in a sheltered spot against a sunny wall. It reaches 6x8 feet. Zones 7–10.

RUDBECKIA (Coneflower, Black-eyed Susan)

The aptly-named black-eyed Susan flowers over a very long period from late summer through early fall. One of the best cultivars is Rudbeckia fulgida sullivantii 'Goldsturm' (zones 4–9), which has stiff upright stems topped with large rich orange-yellow daisy flowers, each with a prominent dark brown cone in the center. In the soft warm light of early fall, the plant absolutely glows in the border. The basal clump of handsome, deep green foliage is also attractive, the lance-shaped leaves being deeply veined. It grows to 24 inches high.

A quite different coneflower is the towering Rudbeckia 'Herbstsonne' (syn. 'Autumn Sun', zones 3–9). This cultivar grows up to 6 feet in height and the long, leafy stems culminate in large golden-yellow blooms with drooping petals surrounding tall, bright green cones. Despite its height, this cultivar rarely needs staking.

Grow rudbeckias on fertile, moisture-retentive ground in a sunny or lightly shaded position. Mulch plants growing on drier soils in spring to conserve moisture and prevent them wilting in the summer months. Deadhead, but leave some dried blooms on 'Goldsturm' for fall decoration.

SALVIA (Ornamental Sage)

There are several excellent hardy herbaceous salvias grown for their summer flowers. One of the earliest to flower is Salvia x sylvestris 'Mainacht' (zones 5–9), measuring 36x18 inches, with many strongly-upright indigo-blue flower spikes. This is followed later in midsummer by the violet-blue Salvia x superba (zones 5–9), which grows to 24x18 inches. The crimson-purple bracts persist long after flowering, extending the season of interest through to September.

Salvia verticillata 'Purple Rain' (zones 6–8) grows to 18x24 inches and blooms mid to late summer with rich purple whorled flowers at regular intervals along the stem, the lush leafy growth forming a good base for the deeply-colored blooms.

The variegated and colored-leaf forms of the evergreen culinary sage, Salvia officinalis (zones 7–8) work well at the front of a sunny border forming spreading hummocks of

Rodgersia aesculifolia

dense foliage. Two of the better ones are 'Icterina' with gold splashed leaves (12x12 inches) and Purpurascens Group with a deep purple suffusion (24 inches high, with a spread of 36 inches).

Plant salvias in well-drained soil in full sun. Cut back the flower spikes as they start to fade to encourage them to form a second crop of flowers.

SAXIFRAGA X URBIUM
(London Pride)

This invaluable shade plant has very attractive, fleshy, evergreen rosettes of tooth-edged leaves and in early summer, airy sprays of very pale pink blooms. It is perfect for edging and works well in a woodland setting as well as an urban one. Plant London pride on moisture-retentive ground. It grows to 10x24 inches. Zones 6–7.

SCABIOSA 'BUTTERFLY BLUE'

A relative newcomer, this diminutive scabious has an exceptionally long flowering period, blooming from July to October, especially when deadheaded.

The small, mauve-blue pincushion flowers are held on wiry stems over a cushion of leaves. 'Pink Mist' is its pink-flowered counterpart. Grow in full sun on light, well-drained soil. It grows to 12x10 inches. Zones 3–8.

SCHIZOSTYLIS COCCINEA (Crimson Flag, Kaffir Lily)

This plant and its cultivars have broad, grassy foliage and stiff spikes of satiny, cup-shaped blooms in a range of colors from white, through pinks and salmon to deep crimson. They begin to flower in fall and some continue well into early winter, weather permitting. For many years, only the satiny, scarlet-red species and the free-flowering cultivars 'Major', 'Viscountess Byng' (pink) and 'Mrs Hegarty' (pale pink) were seen in gardens. Recent breeding has produced a whole clutch of excellent cultivars.

Sedum 'Herbstfreude' (syn. 'Autumn Joy')

Some of the best are 'Sunrise' (large salmon-pink blooms), 'Jennifer' (large soft pink flowers), 'Professor Barnard' (dusky pink), 'Fenland Daybreak' (satin pink) and 'November Cheer' (clear pink). In their native South Africa, Schizostylis experience plentiful summer rain and relatively dry winters. So, to get the best from plants, they need to be grown in full sun on fertile, moisture-retentive soil that does not suffer from prolonged waterlogging in winter. Divide clumps every few years. In cold areas protect with a mulch piled over the crown. Plants reach 24x10 inches. Zones 7–9.

SEDUM (Stonecrop)

These succulent-leaved plants are drought resistant and do well in hot, sunny areas tolerating poor, dry soils. They have a very long season of interest and are grown both for their attractive foliage and their flowers that appear between midsummer and fall. Leaves can be green, often with purple or red suffusions, silver or blue-gray through to darkest maroon purple as in Sedum telephium maximum 'Atropurpureum' (zones 4–9) and the new S. t. 'Matrona'. There are mat-forming alpines, to 36-inch high herbaceous perennials, but there are many in the low to mid range that are ideal for path edging and front-of-the-border positions. For a carpet of purple-blue foliage smothered in purplish-red flowers through the fall, choose 'Bertram Anderson' (zones 5–9) which measures 4x12 inches. 'Ruby Glow' (zones 5–9) is also dark and measures 8x10 inches, while 'Vera Jameson' (zones 4–9) has paler dusky pink blooms and reaches 8x12 inches.

The tiny, star-like flowers are usually held in tight clusters, and in several of the larger cultivars, form domed heads reminiscent of broccoli florets. In Sedum spectabile 'Brilliant' (rose pink, zones 4–9), the new cultivars S. 'Gooseberry Fool' (green and cream) and 'Stewed Rhubarb Mountain' (pink and cream), and the brick-pink 'Herbstfreude' (syn.'Autumn Joy', zones 3–10), these flower heads add sculptural interest long before their official flowering period in late summer and fall.

SISYRINCHIUM STRIATUM

This species produces iris-like fans of gray-green leaves above which robust stems carry small, rounded, cream blooms from mid- to late summer. It self-seeds readily in the border or into gravel. This evergreen is relatively short lived, but its life may be prolonged by dividing it in late summer.

In the cultivar 'Aunt May', the leaves are striped with cream making the perfect foil for the flowers. These are plants for a hot, sunny spot with good winter drainage – a gravel garden would be ideal. Remove dead flower stems and leaves to keep plants looking fresh through the season. It grows to 24 inches high. Zones 7–8.

STACHYS (Lamb's Ears)

The common name perfectly describes the soft rounded leaves that are covered in silken, silvery-gray hairs. This evergreen makes an excellent front-of-the-border plant and the ordinary Stachys byzantina (zones 4–8) throws up leafy upright flower spikes during summer that bear magenta-pink blooms that are almost lost in the woolly coating. It works particularly well with catmint (Nepeta) as a foreground to roses. Plants grow to 16x20 inches. 'Cotton Boll' has stems bearing silvery-white bobbles (24x20 inches) and 'Primrose Heron' is grown for its pale greenish-yellow foliage that gradually changes as summer progresses, becoming silvery-gray in winter. It reaches 18x24 inches. The best non-flowering form is 'Silver Carpet'. These plants are easy to grow in any free-drained soil in full sun.

Another ground cover plant, this time with scalloped-edged glossy green leaves, is Stachys macrantha, big betony (zones 5–7). In early to midsummer, it produces short fat spikes of mauve-pink flowers. 'Robusta' has deeper-colored, more compact flower heads and grows to 24x18 inches. Unlike lamb's ears, this plant does best on moisture-retentive soil and will tolerate light shade.

STIPA (Feather Grass)

Stipa gigantea forms a dense clump of grass-like evergreen leaves 24 inches high and in early summer sends up 6-foot stems bearing oat-like flower sprays. These shimmer gold in sunlight and are long lasting. It makes a superb specimen for the gravel garden and works well in a border where the airy flower sprays lighten heavier planting.

S. calamagrostis (zones 7–10) flowers from midsummer to fall. The arching sheaves of greenish-white flowers, growing up to 4 feet, gradually turn buff, retaining a satin sheen that catches the light. It is lovely as a backdrop to more "solid" flowers. It forms similar basal clumps of leaves to S. gigantea. Grow these grasses in full sun on any well-drained soil.

SYMPHYTUM (Ornamental Comfrey)

The common comfrey is a rampant colonizer, but several less vigorous plants are suitable for the semi-wild shade garden or as ground cover under trees. Symphytum 'Goldsmith' (zones 5–9) has large soft leaves with a broad and irregular gold and cream margin, a lovely foil for its blue and white hanging bell flowers. It grows to 12 inches in height.

Better known is the white-margined S. x uplandicum 'Variegatum' (zones 3–9). Its flowers are blue and pink carried on variegated stems. It reaches 36x24 inches. S. 'Hidcote Pink' (zones 5–9) is a green-leaved cultivar with the flowers opening to hanging bells of pink and white. 'Hidcote Blue' is similar, but with red buds opening to soft blue and aging to white. It reaches 18x18 inches. Both plants make superb ground cover for shade beneath trees or shrubs, tolerating even dry conditions. A good white-flowered species to choose for a similar site is S. orientale (30x18 inches). The variegated cultivars like a cool, moisture-retentive fertile soil and a site sheltered from strong winds and direct sun that can scorch the leaves. Otherwise these ornamental comfreys are trouble free.

THYMUS (Thyme)

These drought-resistant, aromatic, evergreen herbs come in a wide variety of forms with tiny leaves making spreading carpets or low hummocks. Foliage can be green, gray and woolly, golden, or variegated yellow or white. Some thymes are grown chiefly for their tiny clustered purple-pink flowers that appear in midsummer and are a

Stachys byzantina 'Silver Carpet'

magnet for bees, others for their foliage. Carpeting thymes are tough and can be planted in cracks in paving to soften the look. Thymes also work well in gravel as a foil for dwarf, early-flowering bulbs, in low walls and in drought-resistant container plantings.

They do best in full sun on well-drained soil. They are moderately hardy, though need replacing from time to time as they get straggly. Some of the variegated and gold-leaved cultivars have a tendency to revert back to a non-variegated form, so remove any plain green shoots that appear.

Thymus x citriodorus 'Aureus' and 'Bertram Anderson' (both zones 6–9) are gold-leaved forms of lemon thyme that need a warm sheltered position. 'Silver Queen' has white variegated leaves and grows to 6x6 inches.

T. 'Doone Valley' covers the ground in an attractive dense carpet 4 inches high, with dark green and golden yellow variegated leaves. Creeping or wild thyme (Thymus serphyllum, zones 4–9) has many good varieties including the bright crimson T. s. coccineus and the cultivar 'Pink Chintz'. It grows to 2x12 inches.

Tricyrtis formosana

TOLMIEA MENZESII 'TAFF'S GOLD' (Piggyback Plant)

Once grown mainly as a houseplant, this yellow-mottled plant is now used for ground cover in woodland or shady borders. The ivy-shaped leaves produce baby plants where the leaf joins the stalk. Insignificant flowers appear in late spring. Grow in shade on moisture-retentive, humus-rich, well-drained soil with a neutral to acid pH. Clumps reach 24x12 inches. Zones 6–9.

TRICYRTIS (Toad Lily)

The late summer or early fall blooms are not showy, but have a subtle beauty with their intriguing shape and mottled colors. The flowers are formed in loose clusters at the top of arching stems. Grow in woodland on moisture-retentive, humus-rich soil. They will sometimes need sunshine to encourage them to flower, especially in cooler regions. The purple-flowered species, Tricyrtis hirta (zones 4–9) which grows 36x24 inches, and T. formosana (zones 6–9, 24x18 inches) are among the best along with the cultivar 'Lilac Towers'. Tricyrtis hirta alba and T. 'White Towers' are pure white and show up well in shade.

TRILLIUM (Wakerobin)

The first thing you notice about these woodlanders is that everything is in threes. Three broad leaves at the end of each stem are surmounted by three petals. All species flower between spring and early summer and require shade and woodland soil – moisture-retentive, rich in humus, with a neutral to slightly acid pH. One of the best is the great white trillium or white wakerobin (Trillium giganteum) that flowers in late spring with white or pink-tinged blooms. It reaches 18x18 inches. Zones 6–9.

VERATRUM NIGRUM (Black Hellebore)

It takes a few years for these choice perennials to establish and begin flowering, but in the meantime, the foliage is immensely decorative. In spring, fans of broad pleated leaves emerge, looking a little like hostas. You need to take as much care as you would for hostas to protect them from slugs and snails. The leaves, strongly upright at first, gradually expand and flatten out, forming clumps around 12 inches high by 24 inches wide. They do best in shade on moisture-retentive soil with plenty of organic matter and annual mulching. The dark purple-brown branched flower spikes reach 6 feet in summer and make long-lasting seed heads. Zones 6–9.

VERBASCUM (Mullein)

These short-lived perennials or biennials send up tall, stately spires of yellow, white, pink, mauve or buff flowers through the summer months. The large basal leaves may be felted with silvery hairs or wool and this coating often extends to the branched flower spires. A good example is Verbascum bombyciferum (zones 4–8), an evergreen with sulfur yellow flowers (V. olympicum, zones 5–9, is similar). The form V. b. 'Polarsommer' ('Arctic Summer') has white blooms and measures 6 foot high.

In the semi-evergreen nettle-leaved mullein, Verbascum chaixii 'Album' (zones 5–9) the spires are again white, but each bloom is marked with a prominent mauve-purple "eye". It grows to 4 feet tall. The Cotswold hybrids contain several fine cultivars for the border including 'Cotswold Beauty', of subtle amber hue (4 feet tall); 'Gainsborough', a soft yellow (5 feet tall); 'Mont Blanc', a silver-white reaching 3 feet and 'Pink Domino', taller at 4 feet, with deep rose-pink blooms highlighted by a darker "eye." They are all hardy in climate zones 5–9. The popular 'Helen Johnson' has very unusual buff-pink blooms, and grows to 4 feet high. Grow on any reasonable, well-drained soil in full sun. Moist, rich soil tends to make plants grow soft and increases the need for staking. Remove faded spikes to encourage further blooms. Although quite tall, these are slender plants and can be used to break up the line at the front of a border. They also look well as focal points in gravel gardens.

VERBENA
(South American Vervain)

Verbena bonariensis (zones 7–11) is a somewhat tender perennial with stiff, wiry branched stems with clusters of tiny lavender-purple scented blooms. Flowering in late summer and fall, it is a magnet for butterflies, bees and hoverflies. The clump of dark green leaves takes up little room and the tall stems are self supporting. Plants are not long lived, but they self-seed. In mild areas, large colonies can build up, creating a purple haze in the border. Grow in full sun on fertile, well-drained soil. Mulch roots in fall to protect from frost. Plants grow to 6 feet high.

Verbena corymbosa (zones 9–11) is a shorter version. It can be invasive on damp soils, but it must have a moisture-retentive soil to really thrive. It grows to 4 feet in height.

VERONICASTRUM
VIRGINICUM ALBUM

In late summer, this architectural plant sends up a series of perfectly-vertical flower stems carrying slender white spikes of tiny blooms. Its lance-shaped leaves are arranged in whorls set at regular intervals along the stem. For dramatic effect, team it up with plants with a strong horizontal profile such as achilleas, or those with rounded foliage, such as sedums. Grow on any fertile, well-drained, moisture-retentive soil, including alkaline ones. It grows to 5 feet high with a spread of about 24 inches. Zones 3–8.

VIOLA

The horned violet, Viola cornuta (zones 7–9), is an evergreen with heart-shaped leaves covered in fragrant blooms of lilac (Lilacina Group) or white (Alba Group) in summer. If the plants are then cut down, fed and watered, flowering resumes in late summer. It makes good ground cover or edging for the front of a shady border where the pale blooms seem to glow.

There are many other hardy viola hybrids and these are often sweetly scented, like the soft-colored 'Belmont Blue'. Colors range from black ('Bowles' Black', zones 4–8) to shades of purple ('Martin' and 'Maggie Mott'), blue ('Belmont Blue') and yellow ('Moonlight'). 'Irish Molly' has beautiful yellow blooms overlaid with bronze.

Grow in sun or light shade on fertile, moisture-retentive but well-drained soil. Deadheading is a tedious job, but helps to prolong flowering and even the life of certain cultivars. Plants reach 6x12 inches.

ZANTEDESCHIA
AETHIOPICA
'CROWBOROUGH'

The sculptural white blooms of calla lily 'Crowborough' appear in succession from early to midsummer above handsome arrow-shaped leaves. This cultivar is hardier than the species, but nevertheless needs a protective mulch over the crown until well established. Grow in shallow water at the edge of a pool, in a bog garden, or in moisture-retentive soil in a sunny or lightly-shaded border. It is also suitable for growing in a pot, but keep well watered. Plants grow to 24x18 inches. Zones 8–10.

Veronicastrum virginicum album

Index

Acknowledgements

The publishers would like to thank the individuals who supplied the photographs on the following pages:

Clive Nichols Garden Pictures: 8; 9 top both; 10 bottom; 11 (with Ulf Nordfjell); 12 (Sticky Wicket, Dorset); 13 bottom (Little Bowden, Berks); 16 (Little Bowden, Berks); 17 left and right (Brook Cottage, Oxon); 19; 25 bottom (Greyston Cottage, Oxon); 32; 37 (Arley Hall, Cheshire); 38 (designer Elizabeth Woodhouse); 46 right (Wollerton Old Hall, Shropshire); 48 center (Rosendal, Sweden); 50 top left (Hadspen Garden, Somerset); 51 (The Anchorage, Kent); 52 top right (Wollerton Old Hall, Shropshire); 53 top (Hadspen Garden, Somerset); 53 bottom; 55 (designers N. Hancock & Mathew Bell); 57 bottom; 58–9 (designer Elizabeth Woodhouse); 59 right (Bosvigo House, Truro, Cornwall); 60 (Chenies Manor, Bucks); 64; 67 (Bassibones Farm, Bucks); 80–1 (The Old Vicarage, Norfolk); 84 (Wollerton Old Hall, Shropshire); 95 top right; 103; 115; 118

John Glover Photography: front jacket; 3; 6; 7 top left; 9 bottom; 10 top; 13 top right; 14; 18; 20–1 both; 22–23 all; 24; 25 top; 31 bottom; 33; 39; 44; 45 top left; 46 left; 47 right; 48 left; 49 right; 50 bottom left; 52–3 center top; 54 top; 57 top; 58; 62; 63 all; 65 all; 66; 68; 69 bottom; 70; 71 both; 75 top; 78; 79 top left and bottom; 81 bottom; 82, 83; 95 top left; 105; 120; 122; 124, 125; 128 bottom; 131, 132; 134; 138

Jenny Hendy: 1; 7 top right; 135

Catriona Tudor Erler: 27 top

All other photographs taken by Neil Sutherland, © Quadrillion Publishing Limited.

The publishers would also like to thank:

Merriments Gardens and Nursery, Hurst Green, East Sussex, UK for kindly allowing us to take the following pictures in their garden: 4; 15; 26; 29 top; 30; 36; 40–1; 48 bottom right; 50 top right and bottom right; 56 left; 72 top; 73; 76 top; 77; 97
Parham Park, Pulborough, West Sussex, UK for allowing us to take the following pictures in their garden: p14; p56–7 center; p72 bottom
Murrell's Plant & Garden Centre, Pulborough, West Sussex for the loan of plants for photography.